Barcode in Back

D1570941

HUMBER LIBRARIES LAKESHORE CAN
3199 Lakeshore Blvd West
TORONTO, ON.   M8V 1K8

The Future of Finance

Founded in 1807, John Wiley & Sons is the oldest independent publishing company in the United States. With offices in North America, Europe, Australia and Asia, Wiley is globally committed to developing and marketing print and electronic products and services for our customers' professional and personal knowledge and understanding.

The Wiley Finance series contains books written specifically for finance and investment professionals as well as sophisticated individual investors and their financial advisors. Book topics range from portfolio management to e-commerce, risk management, financial engineering, valuation and financial instrument analysis, as well as much more.

For a list of available titles, please visit our Web site at www .WileyFinance.com.

The Future of Finance

A New Model for Banking and Investment

MOORAD CHOUDHRY
GINO LANDUYT

WILEY

John Wiley & Sons, Inc.

HUMBER LIBRARIES LAKESHORE CAMPUS
3199 Lakeshore Blvd West
TORONTO, ON.   M8V 1K8

Copyright © 2010 by Moorad Choudhry and Gino Landuyt. All rights reserved.

Published by John Wiley & Sons, Inc., Hoboken, New Jersey.
Published simultaneously in Canada.

No part of this publication may be reproduced, stored in a retrieval system, or transmitted in any form or by any means, electronic, mechanical, photocopying, recording, scanning, or otherwise, except as permitted under Section 107 or 108 of the 1976 United States Copyright Act, without either the prior written permission of the Publisher, or authorization through payment of the appropriate per-copy fee to the Copyright Clearance Center, Inc., 222 Rosewood Drive, Danvers, MA 01923, (978) 750-8400, fax (978) 646-8600, or on the Web at www.copyright.com. Requests to the Publisher for permission should be addressed to the Permissions Department, John Wiley & Sons, Inc., 111 River Street, Hoboken, NJ 07030, (201) 748-6011, fax (201) 748-6008, or online at http://www.wiley.com/go/permissions.

Limit of Liability/Disclaimer of Warranty: While the publisher and author have used their best efforts in preparing this book, they make no representations or warranties with respect to the accuracy or completeness of the contents of this book and specifically disclaim any implied warranties of merchantability or fitness for a particular purpose. No warranty may be created or extended by sales representatives or written sales materials. The advice and strategies contained herein may not be suitable for your situation. You should consult with a professional where appropriate. Neither the publisher nor author shall be liable for any loss of profit or any other commercial damages, including but not limited to special, incidental, consequential, or other damages.

Author's Disclaimer: This book does not constitute investment advice and its contents should not be construed as such. The contents should not be considered as a recommendation to deal and the authors do not accept liability for actions resulting from a reading of any material in this book.

While every effort has been made to ensure accuracy, no responsibility for loss occasioned to any person acting or refraining from action as a result of any material in this book can be accepted by the authors, publisher, or any named person or corporate entity.

The material in this book is based on information that is considered reliable, but neither the author nor the publishers warrant that it is accurate or complete, and it should not be relied on as such. Opinions expressed are current opinions only and are subject to change. The author and publishers are not soliciting any action based upon this material. Moorad Choudhry, Gino Landuyt, and any named person or entity may or may not have a position in any capital market instrument described in this book, at the time of writing or subsequently. Any such position is subject to change at any time and for any reason.

For general information on our other products and services or for technical support, please contact our Customer Care Department within the United States at (800) 762-2974, outside the United States at (317) 572-3993 or fax (317) 572-4002.

Wiley also publishes its books in a variety of electronic formats. Some content that appears in print may not be available in electronic books. For more information about Wiley products, visit our web site at www.wiley.com.

Library of Congress Cataloging-in-Publication Data:

Choudhry, Moorad.
   The future of finance : a new model for banking and investment / Moorad Choudhry, Gino Landuyt.
      p. cm. – (Wiley finance series)
   Includes bibliographical references and index.
   ISBN 978-0-470-57229-0
   1. Banks and banking.   2. Portfolio management.   3. Risk.   4. Investments.   5. Global Financial Crisis, 2008-2009.   I. Landuyt, Gino.   II. Title.
   HG1573.C44 2010
   332.1–dc22

                                                                              2010018129

Printed in the United States of America

10 9 8 7 6 5 4 3 2 1

HUMBER LIBRARIES LAKESHORE CAMPUS
3199 Lakeshore Blvd West
TORONTO, ON.   M8V 1K3

*Dedicated to the spirit of John Lennon, Paul McCartney,
George Harrison, and Ringo Starr—masters in the pursuit of excellence.
—Moorad Choudhry*

*In loving memory of my grandmother (June 21, 1915–May 1, 2009)
—Gino Landuyt*

Contents

Foreword

Economic and financial crashes are nothing new. Students of finance will be familiar with the pattern of crises that has beset markets since the 1700s. However, the crisis of 2007–2009 was unique in certain respects. First, it took place in an era of globalization, with its consequent almost instantaneous transmission of events. Second, it followed no set pattern. There was no initial shock followed by recovery; rather, economies and markets were beset by a series of shocks, each of greater impact than the last. Thus, the initial events—the crisis in the U.S. subprime residential mortgage market, the losses at two Bear Stearns hedge funds, the illiquidity in the asset-backed commercial paper market, the run on the UK bank Northern Rock—led seemingly to a still greater crisis, culminating in the bankruptcy of Lehman Brothers and the government bailout of the insurance giant American Insurance Group (AIG). It was at this point that governments in the United States and Europe had to step in and save their banking sectors from imminent collapse. The crisis of 2007–2009 differed from previous market corrections in that for a time there appeared to be no end in sight for it.

The near failure of the banking system and the worldwide recession that followed provoked considerable debate on how it had been allowed to happen, and what steps should be taken to reduce the likelihood of another crash and, if such a crash should occur, how to mitigate taxpayer exposure. It was evident that egregious errors had been made in bank governance, regulatory policy, and risk management regimes. The diversity of firms impacted by the crash, however, suggests there is no simple, universal cure for the financial markets. Banks and investors are better advised to learn the lessons of the crash and adopt policies and processes that mitigate the effects of the next crash, rather than think that they can avoid its impact altogether.

The financial crash and its aftermath have already been covered extensively in the literature. Academics, practitioners, and journalists have provided the market with numerous treatises and analyses, some of it polemic in nature and all too often offering little added value. Wisdom in hindsight is abundant. When we remember that John Kenneth Galbraith's seminal study of the 1929 stock market crash was published 25 years after the event, it is clear that the lessons to be learned from the latest crash will take some time to formulate and digest; much of the material published so far on the crash suffers from being written in haste, and that brings me to this present work by Moorad Choudhry and Gino Landuyt. The authors have benefited from taking a longer term perspective at the causal factors behind the crash, and this has paid off in the value and tractability of their policy recommendations. They point out the paradox of financial markets: unlike many other asset types, an increase in financial asset prices leads to increasing demand. A proper understanding of the markets, and how to position oneself for changes in conditions throughout the economic cycle, will serve bank boards and investors best.

Another lesson of the crisis, which Messrs. Choudhry and Landuyt point out, is that market stability itself plants the seeds of the next crisis. In an environment of stable interest rates, low inflation, and economic growth, banks and leveraged investors extend their risk-reward frontiers and take on more debt. This makes sense if one makes an implicit assumption that growth will be continuous, and that asset prices will only move upwards. But to make this assumption is to be unprepared for the inevitable downturn. The paradox of stable markets needs to be built in to any practical implementation of efficient market theory and modern portfolio theory. The authors review the conundrums at hand, and list practical steps that investors can take in their approach to more efficient fund management. The crisis of 2008 was also a crisis in bank liquidity; helpfully, this book reviews liquidity policy and how banks can set up a more effective liquidity risk management infrastructure.

I have known and worked with Dr. Choudhry for ten years, and it is a pleasure to write this Foreword. Investors will find much valuable insight in this succinct and accessible book, as well as recommendations of practical import to take with them into the changed, more risk-averse era of finance.

Frank J. Fabozzi
Professor in the Practice of Finance, Yale School of Management
Editor, *Journal of Portfolio Management*
July 2010

Preface

The year 2008 was an *annus horribilis* for investors in financial markets. No investor was protected against the downfall in asset prices. Even the stars of the past decade, the wizards of Greenwich who promised that investment portfolios would be made immune to downward correction by adding portable alpha to their portfolios, had to admit that there was no safe haven. Diversification across several different asset classes didn't work either, since every major asset class appeared to be under attack.

What the 2007–2009 credit crunch and economic recession reminded us was that diversification and the efficient portfolio theory do not apply at all times. What is apparent is that a cornerstone of modern finance, the modern portfolio theory (MPT), did not withstand the test during the financial market crisis of 2007–2008. Moreover, in a bear market it can be observed that diversification to hedge or spread risk sometimes destroys value rather than creates it, because it merely magnifies the existing risk exposure for no further reward.

Consider the Credit Suisse/Tremont Hedge Fund Index returns in Table P.1 (also shown in Chapter 6 as Table 6.1). All the strategies shown (except for dedicated shorts and managed futures) reported a negative performance for 2008. We can argue that both dedicated shorts and managed futures are pure directional plays, like betting in a casino, and anticipate a negative downturn, and so would always perform positively in a bearish environment. These two strategies cannot be said to represent the application of MPT.

The problem is that MPT and the diversification argument, like so many good investment ideas, only work in a bull market, when investors pay at least lip service to "fundamentals" and attempt to apply some logic in share valuation. In a bear market, or in any period of negative sentiment, all asset prices and markets go down. And in times of crises, as we have observed during 2007–2008, correlation between asset classes is practically unity.

It does not matter what industry, country, or level of managerial expertise is being considered; all prices go down and all credit spreads widen in a bear market such as the one we experienced in the recent crisis. In that crisis, everyone lost money: banks, hedge funds, volatility traders, private

TABLE P.1 Credit Suisse/Tremont Hedge Fund Index Performance 2008

	Index Value		Return		YTD
	Dec-08	Nov-08	Dec-08	Nov-08	
Credit Suisse/Tremont Hedge Fund Index	351.08	351.2	−0.03%	−4.15%	−19.07%
Convertible Arbitrage	221.62	223.82	−0.98%	−1.88%	−31.59%
Dedicated Short Bias	88.94	90.46	−1.68%	3.04%	14.87%
Emerging Markets	264.49	263.92	0.22%	−1.87%	−30.41%
Equity Market Neutral	225.47	224.54	0.41%	−40.85%	−40.32%
Event Driven:	395.52	400.56	−1.26%	−3.21%	−17.74%
Distressed	452.18	463.96	−2.54%	−5.00%	−20.48%
Multi-Strategy	371.03	372.86	−0.49%	−2.17%	−16.25%
Risk Arbitrage	277.63	273.26	1.60%	−0.02%	−3.27%
Fixed Income Arbitrage	166.79	168.13	−0.80%	−5.60%	−28.82%
Global Macro	582.69	576.3	1.11%	1.54%	−4.62%
Long/Short Equity	401.98	397.78	1.06%	−1.41%	−19.76%
Managed Futures	284.19	277.61	2.37%	3.22%	18.33%
Multi-Strategy	275.79	280.04	−1.52%	−4.63%	−23.63%

Note: All currencies in USD.
Source: Credit Suisse/Tremont Hedge Funds Index. Reproduced with permission.

equity, long/short investors, and traditional long-only fund managers all registered losses.[1] More significantly, if we look closer at the Credit Suisse/ Tremont Index we notice that even the long/short equity index is down in this period as well, by over 30 percent. This refutes the claim that these strategies generated alpha.

On paper, diversification principles carry elegance and neatness but where modern portfolio theory suffers the greatest weakness is in its assumption that in every market, correlation is below 1.00. What we have observed over the past five years, whether it is managed on the basis of fundamental factors, momentum, arbitrage, or any other rationale, is that everything tends to end up on the same side of the trade at the same time. Believers in portfolio theory are convinced that (for instance) alternative investments are somehow negatively correlated with basic equities. During 2007–2008 they learned the hard way that this was simply not true. Bonds, equities, commodities, and currencies aren't asset classes in their own right.

The same argument applies to banks that diversified by branching out and operating globally. The rationale was that moving into different geographical regions spread and diversified risk. In fact all this did was magnify risk across economies so that when the credit crunch came it hit them everywhere. While the ultimate global bank, HSBC, weathered the storm fairly well despite its geographical dispersion, due largely to its conservative liquidity management policy and strong capital base, some of the largest losses, in relative terms, occurred at global banks such as Citibank, RBS, and UBS.

The efficient market hypothesis and MPT clearly had their merits over the past 35 years. They were the basis for an investment and banking model that generated significant returns from the 1980s onward. However, in a severe bear market this philosophy has been seen to be flawed, and contributed to the development of a banking business model that suffered large losses. The inaccurate assumptions on which it is based suggest that a paradigm shift in economics needs to take place that modifies or completely replaces MPT. Portfolio diversification only makes sense if one has the possibility of picking out assets which are uncorrelated. Unfortunately, in a severe recessionary environment, correlation tends to go to one within every asset class, so this is a nonstarter for anything other than a short-term (less than five-year) investment horizon.

Our suggestion is that the paradigm shift in financial economics should be a reversion to traditional markets. Not only does diversifying across asset classes and geographical regions *not* spread risk, in a bear market it actually amplifies risk. The clear lesson from the crisis is to know one's risk, and that is best done by concentrating on assets and sectors that one is familiar with. Diversifying in the name of the MPT will only erode value.

Some of our policy recommendations include the advice to:

- Restructure the business model to assets and regions in which one has genuine understanding and expertise.
- For banks, secure long-term liquidity to allow for times of market corrections and illiquidity. We further recommend avoiding overleveraging on the capital base.

These and other recommendations are explored in detail in Part Two of this book. In essence, we hope to demonstrate our belief that a paradigm shift that results in a greater concentration on familiarity and an acceptance of lower average returns will do much to prevent large-scale losses at the time of the next market correction.

This book reviews the causes and consequences of the financial market crash of 2007–2009, and presents recommendations on how to create a more sustainable bank and investment model for the future. Specifically, we look at how banks should be structured and governed, particularly with regard to their liquidity risk management and board corporate governance, and at a set of investment guidelines that would be least susceptible to the next market crash. Highlights of Part One of the book include a wide-ranging review of the causes of the financial crash, and note that many of the causal factors behind it remain in place. Part Two of the book presents our recommendations for a revised model for both banking and principles of investment, which we believe, if followed, will produce a more sustainable business environment.

Crashes of one sort or another are an integral part of the free-market economy. Rather than trying to prevent them or, worse still, thinking that they can be avoided or legislated away, it behooves financial market practitioners and regulators to place themselves and the firms in which they work in a position where they suffer least from the impact of crashes when they do occur. We believe that implementing some of the recommendations in this book will assist firms to achieve this goal.

Moorad Choudhry
Surrey, England
April 2010

Gino Landuyt
London, England
April 2010

The spread of secondary and tertiary education has created a large population of people, often with well-developed literary and scholarly tastes, who have been educated far beyond their capacity to undertake analytical thought.

—Peter Medawar, quoted in R. Dawkins,
The Greatest Show on Earth:
The Evidence for Evolution
(London: Bantam Press, 2009)

Introduction

The financial markets have always been plagued by crises and bubbles of one sort or another. Students of economic history will be familiar with the South Sea Bubble, the Dutch Tulip Bubble, and the Wall Street crash of 1929, as well as more recent events such as the 1997 Asian currency crisis and the 1998 bailout by the U.S. Federal Reserve of the hedge fund Long Term Capital Management (LTCM). Crashes are nothing new and, far from being viewed as something rare or odd, should instead be viewed as the norm, and inherent to the nature of free markets. Finance has always suffered from crises, and this is true irrespective of whether the financial system in place is open or closed, simple or sophisticated.

Financial markets promised prosperity, and in large part they delivered, especially in the postwar period. The impact of the adoption of managed floating foreign exchange rates, free movement of capital, and a host of other free market principles has been an exponential rise in prosperity and human economic development, all over the world. If one wants to observe the end result of the application of technology that has been made possible solely via the availability of large-scale, cross-border finance, then look no further than one's cellular phone. When one sees a rickshaw puller on the streets of Dhaka, earning an average salary of $1.00 per day, and using a mobile phone, one is observing the obvious, material benefit to humankind of the free market in banking and finance. The development of affordable, accessible mobile phone telephony would not have been possible without the existence of global banking and securitization markets to provide the billions of dollars necessary to finance the mobile phone companies' research and development process. The benefits of financial markets are many and all around us.

During 2007–2008, however, the structure and behavior of the financial markets themselves caused an implosion that resulted in a banking crisis, recession, and much human misery. Certain financial instruments, the more sophisticated ones, were viewed in the mainstream media as being part of the problem. *CDO* (meaning collateralized debt obligation) became a household term and a byword for seemingly bad practice. In fact, losses suffered by banks were highest in another category of structured finance product, the mortgage-backed security, but that is beside the point.

In essence, it is the inherent nature of the markets themselves that makes them prone to busts after a boom, as part of a cyclical process. Let's consider some salient points now.

MARKET INSTABILITY

Free movement of capital is the cornerstone of the Anglo-Saxon financial market model. This in itself can create problems over the long term. In an earlier era, after the 1973–1974 oil shock that resulted in a fourfold increase in the price of oil, the oil-exporting countries found themselves sitting on large pools of U.S. dollar foreign exchange reserves. This they placed on deposit at Western banks, creating a large cash surplus for said banks. The banks needed to put this cash to work, which is understandable because (1) they need to generate return to enable them to pay deposit interest, and (2) the balance sheet has to balance—the OPEC liabilities needed to be lent out as assets. Many of these *petrodollars* were therefore lent to Latin American and other sovereign governments, and the rest, as they say, is history: The countries either defaulted on this debt or were close to default, and to prevent a wholesale crash of the U.S. banking system, the U.S. Treasury Secretary, Nicholas Brady, came up with a plan in 1989 (the famous Brady bonds) to save it. Sound familiar? Around the same time, Secretary Brady was also behind the plan to bail out the U.S. savings and loan banking sector, which eventually cost the U.S. taxpayer $124 billion. Again, a familiar process.

In the most recent crisis, capital inflows can be seen to be part of the originating causal factors. Excess foreign exchange reserves from Asian and oil-exporting countries, most significantly China, were placed in the West, either directly via holdings of government bonds, principally U.S. Treasuries, or at Western banks. For example:

- The United States between 2000 and 2008 received $5.7 trillion, equal to 40 percent of its 2007 GDP.
- The United Kingdom and Ireland received over 20 percent of their combined 2007 GDP as foreign reserves investment from exporting countries.
- Spain received over 50 percen8t of its GDP in such investments.

By any standards these are large infusions of cash. What is the impact of such capital inflows? Well, the full impact is large, but it is apparent that some of the results of this abundance of funds, especially in the banking sector, were that (1) credit becomes cheaper and domestic savings decline; (2) assets prices are driven up, partly due to the availability of cheap credit; and (3) there is a housing boom.

The four countries named earlier all experienced housing booms and busts during the period 2002–2008.

We stated right at the beginning, in the Preface, that economic downturns and crashes are an inherent part of the free-market system. In that respect, the events of 2007–2008 are nothing new. They do have a unique feature, however, and that is the speed at which the crisis unfolded. Globalization, the instant electronic transmission of money, the Internet— these are all features of the crash of the past decade. The instantaneous nature of the financial market, worldwide, is a structural feature that aided the generation and transmission of the crisis, and will do so again. It is a fact peculiar to the financial industry. An industrial corporation, for example, must build its plant, rent space, hire workers, and so on, all of which takes time. In finance one can deal—and suffer the consequences— right away. This aspect helps fuel a boom.

Consider also the following peculiar and virtually unique feature of finance: It is the only industry in which rising prices lead to higher demand. In almost every other industry, such as automobiles, energy, airlines, white goods, and a whole host of other sectors, holding all else equal, if the price of the product goes up demand will fall. This isn't so in finance. Here, people treat rising asset prices differently: Rising prices lead to *increased* demand! As equity or house prices rise, more and more customers, the investors, start to pile into the product. When prices fall, investors pull out, often at a loss. Financial assets are virtually the only asset class or commodity for which rising prices lead to increased demand. This paradox of finance helps fuel an asset price boom and inevitable bust.

Tie this in with the first factor noted earlier, the availability of easy and cheap credit, and the ingredients of the boom start to fall into place. As prices rise, credit becomes more abundant. This fuels the boom—and everyone, including retail buyers and politicians, enjoys a boom. Hence, regulatory and policy actions that might constrain a boom, such as increased regulation or a rise in interest rates, become difficult to implement. Finally, financial stability itself during an era of rising prices fuels a boom.[1] This breeds confidence and increases the level of risk taking. In other words, just as one should start to become more risk-averse as the market reaches ever higher highs, risk aversion starts diminishing and investors take on ever more risk and make bigger bets.

DERIVATIVES AND MATHEMATICAL MODELING

In 1998 the hedge fund LTCM imploded in a deluge of losses on its trades and had to be bailed out by the U.S. Federal Reserve, which worried about the systemic risk arising from a failure of the fund, given that its counter-parties included many major U.S. banks. LTCM was an example of the use of high leverage; at the time of its demise it was said that the debt-to-equity ratio of the fund was around 100:1. In 2008 Lehman Brothers was lever-aged at between 40:1 to 50:1 when it went bust. Excessive leverage is a recipe for disaster. When everyone trades the same way, it creates a crisis. In 1998 LTCM's positions were not replicated by hundreds of large banks all around the world; in 2008 one could not say the same.

In a crisis, correlation is virtually 1.00. This is a danger that arises when everyone piles into one asset class and that asset class goes bad: There is nowhere to turn to except the government. This is an example of *reflexivity*: For example, once people believe that house prices will never fall, they will all get into this asset class and end up buying too much property; at that point, house prices will fall. So, while investment funds believe that diver-sification always pays, they will all invest in the same product and instru-ments. At that point diverse markets cease to be that diverse and actually have something in common: the investment funds that bought into them!

For 2007–2008 that asset was the housing market, and the instrument that helped banks share the benefits was the mortgage-backed security (MBS) and its derivative cousin, the collateralized debt obligation (CDO). Now, MBSs had been around since at least 1979, if not earlier; CDOs dated from about 1998. But what made this time different was that the underlying asset class (mortgage loans) failed, and it was only at this point that inves-tors, which included banks, realized that their lack of understanding of how MBSs and CDOs were modeled was an issue.

The statistical modeling used to value (and rate) CDOs was seen to be inaccurate. The same was true for MBSs. Rating agencies had applied quantitative analysis and statistical modeling as part of their rating process to CDOs. Unlike a corporation, which is subject to qualitative analysis when its debt is being rated (such as the quality of its management, its position versus peer-group competitors, and so on), a CDO can only be rated quantitatively. There is no "qualitative" analysis that can be applied, and which would influence the rating, because, unlike a corporation, a CDO is simply a brass plate on a wall.

Unfortunately, CDO quantitative analysts and the rating agencies did not take into account—partly because their methodology can't actually account for it—falling mortgage underwriting standards. The increasing amount of "self-certified" mortgages were not accounted for in valuation models. This made credit rating levels awarded during 2006 and 2007, when the U.S mortgage market was reaching its peak and loan origination standards were at their lowest, particularly inaccurate guides. The method-ology used, which investors should have done more to understand, had assumed perpetually rising house prices, or at least no fall in house prices, and historical default rates, which unfortunately were about to rise. And once rates rose, the investor lost his proverbial shirt. In a rating agency model, a BBB-rated tranche will pay out at (say) 6 percent default but not at 6.5 percent (although this is irrelevant where secondary market liquidity dries up). Hence, one fraction over the tranche attachment point and the investor has lost his capital.

The conclusion from this experience is that mathematics can only take an investor so far; there remains a big role for judgment and intuition, and this was forgotten at many banks.

SENIOR MANAGEMENT AND STAYING IN THE GAME

At most times, during both a bear market and a bull market, both investors and senior management display a herd mentality that makes bucking the prevailing trend difficult. In a booming market, those who urge restraint or conservatism are often ignored, or simply excluded altogether. The most famous quote that (inadvertently) revealed this mentality came from Chuck Prince, former CEO of Citigroup, who stated in an interview with the *Financial Times* in July 2007, "When the music stops, in terms of liquidity, things will be complicated. But as long as the music is playing, you've got to get up and dance. We're still dancing."

One month later the U.S. subprime crisis broke when investors pulled out of the asset-backed commercial paper market, triggering the start of the interbank liquidity crisis. As for Mr. Prince and Citigroup—well, the rest is history.

Perhaps the fact that managers don't own the firm (the age-old agent-principal argument and a well-studied subject in industrial economics) leads to excessive risk taking. But consider the following: The CEO of Lehman Brothers, Dick Fuld, owned millions of the firm's shares, as did many of the employees, at the time of the firm's collapse. Much of the bonus payment at the company was paid in shares in the company.

MACROPRUDENTIAL FINANCIAL REGULATION AND CYCLE-PROOF REGULATION

Perhaps a starting point for financial market regulators should be an acceptance that crashes and crises in markets are an inherent part of the system. They should be expected, if not every year then at least every decade. There is no point in attempting to prevent banks from failing or asset bubbles from bursting, because this is futile. Rather, the emphasis should be on mitigating the impact on the rest of the market when such events do occur. In other words, regulation can never be infallible, given the inherent market instability.

Another of the causal factors of the crash was the buildup of an unregulated *shadow banking* system, which regulators did not keep up with. This included:

- Hedge funds.
- Special purpose vehicles (SPVs), used to implement all manner of structured finance transactions, including structured investment vehicles (SIVs), collateralized debt obligations (CDOs), and asset-backed commercial paper vehicles (ABCPs).
- Nonbank institutions acting in a bank-like manner, such as GE Capital and AIG.

Regulators did not monitor these vehicles or firms, and in the case of SIVs and ABCP conduits they were ignoring a significant liquidity and credit risk exposure for banks that were kept off the balance sheet, via the SPVs. In addition, while hedge funds cannot be said to have caused the crash, they remain big players in the markets and ones that represent significant counterparty risk for banks.

Regulation is always strengthened in the midst of a bust. Ironically, faith in draconian regulation is strongest at the bottom of the cycle, when there is little need for participants to be regulated (because risk aversion self-regulates them). The paradox is that demand for stringent regulation is at its weakest at the top of an economic cycle, which is precisely when it is most needed—when bank loan origination standards are at their weakest.

To make regulation countercyclical, it needs to be (1) comprehensive, (2) contingent, and (3) cost-effective. Rules that apply comprehensively to all leveraged financial firms are likely to discourage the drift from heavily regulated to lightly regulated firms during a boom. Regulations should be contingent so that they have the most force when the private sector is most likely to do itself harm (during a boom) but impose fewer restrictions at other times. Of course, the problem is deciding exactly what type of economy we are in at any time! Perhaps central banks and regulators can use a range of market indicators and metrics when assessing whether the economy is in danger of overheating?

As for the form of regulations, it may be that instead of firms having to raise permanent capital it is better to have them arrange for capital to be infused when they or the system is in trouble. This would take the form of so-called contingent-capital instruments, such as debt that automatically converts to participating equity when both of two conditions are met: The system is in crisis and the bank's capital ratio falls below a certain value. Another version of such a capital requirement would be to buy collateralized insurance policies (from the government or from foreign investors) that capitalize the firm when it gets into trouble.

Banks' capital is another area for reform. Capital needs to be made *countercyclical* so that it is built up during periods of economic stability, ready to act as a stronger buffer when times turn bad. But there are market arguments about why forcing banks to hold more capital than necessary in a boom is distortional: Business will (as it did in the shadow banking system) move to areas where capital can be reduced.

THE WAY FORWARD

One of the first impacts of the crisis was deleveraging of banks. This was of course a long overdue process. For instance, Lehman Brothers was leveraged at between 40 to 50 times its capital base at the time of its collapse. In the wake of its bankruptcy, banks started to reign in lending and build up their capital base, a natural reaction to a crash.

The preceding narrative gives some flavor of the issues and problems raised by the financial crisis. The final impact on financial markets remains to be seen. In the rest of this book we present recommendations for fixing finance and placing the markets on a firmer footing to withstand the effect of future crises. In the first instance we recommend reregulating finance. A sample of our recommendations includes the following:

- Do away with separate bodies regulating the industry, and merge them into one institution.
- Review the UK Financial Services Authority and Bank of England debate: It makes sense for the regulator to also be the supervisor and lender of last resort (LOLR) for the banking sector.
- Remove tax relief in the mortgage market, to stop fueling a housing boom. Three of the four countries noted earlier for their housing market collapses had such a tax in place (the exception was the United Kingdom, which removed mortgage tax relief some years ago).
- Require all over-the-counter (OTC) derivatives including credit default swaps (CDS) to trade through a central clearinghouse.
- Regulate all firms: no more shadow banks. Put another way, if an entity acts like a bank, and/or engages in leveraged finance, then it should be regulated as a bank.

- Bonuses should be paid more in equity, and a part of it should be made repayable if the recipient's department subsequently loses money. But note that the bonus issue is a red herring—bank remuneration policy didn't cause the crash.
- Only pay a bonus if the bank as a whole makes money: This is economic sense and also fosters more of a team culture.

And above all, address bank liquidity. Liquidity is the water of life of the financial markets.

CONCLUSION

As a rule, innovation in any industry, including finance, is a source of greater wealth. We should not seek to constrain it. Rather, all market participants should seek to understand it better. Financial crises are an unavoidable aspect of the free market. A glance at history will easily confirm this. So before we can tackle mitigating the impact of these crises, we must accept this fact. A boom will always follow a bust, and risk aversion will disappear during the boom . . . so be ready for the consequences of that when the inevitable bust follows!

ONE

A Review of the Financial Crash

Part One of the book is a wide-ranging review of the 2007–2009 financial crisis. It looks beyond the headlines and the media hype to present a full analysis of the factors leading to the crash of 2007 and the banking crisis of 2008, and the interaction between these factors. An understanding of these factors is vital as the first step to designing a banking and investment model that is better placed to withstand the impacts of the next crash in the economic cycle.

CHAPTER 1

Globalization, Emerging Markets, and the Savings Glut

The purpose of this book is to explain the financial crisis from a banking point of view, and to offer solutions for improvement such that the financial industry is better placed to withstand the impact of future crises. Surprising as it may seem, the topics of globalization, emerging markets, and the savings glut cannot be excluded from this book. Often in the search for the causes of the financial crash of 2007–2009, globalization and the role of the Asian and oil-exporting countries are underestimated. In many analyses of the crisis, the successive emerging-market crises over the past decade and the undervalued currency of emerging-market economies gets credited with, at best, only a secondary role in the crisis.

This is to miss a fundamental aspect and causal factor of the crash, and one that had been building up for over a decade. We want to phrase it even more strongly. One of the biggest challenges that world political leaders will be facing in the next decade is to address the global imbalances that have been created over the previous decade. If they do not succeed in this, then even the most robust banking regulation will not be sufficient to protect the financial industry from another financial crisis, the effects of which could be even worse than the one just experienced. In saying this, we recognize the role emerging markets played and are still playing as pivotal to the crash.

GLOBALIZATION

In identifying the responsibility of these emerging-market economies we need to go back to the very beginning of globalization. As we illustrate, the impact of globalization was detrimental in the way it drastically changed the landscape of financial markets. The seeds of globalization were planted at the end of the 1970s. Prior to this the United States possessed something more akin to an autarkic economy than a truly integrated open economy (the United Kingdom, for example, has always been more of an open trading economy than the United States). Apart from dependence, to some extent, on imported oil, the U.S. economy was financed by its own pool of money.

The collapse of the Bretton Woods currency arrangement and the oil shock of 1973–1974 were the first steps leading to an integrated global economy. A major event in the opening up of financial markets in the United States was the broadening of the investment guidelines of pension funds. These were allowed to invest in smaller mid-cap companies, which was the spark for the growth of venture capitalism. The introduction of 401(k) pension schemes freed up more capital and by the mid-1980s, during the Reagan administration, cross-border capital flows started to accelerate. The fall of the Berlin Wall and the collapse of communism in general opened up trade opportunities across the globe, and companies and banks started to operate more internationally. The impact of the implosion of communism was significant, as it released a *peace dividend* as capital previously allocated to defense spending during the Cold War was now able to be invested in free markets. This peace dividend contributed to a liberalization of international trade and increased productivity.

The banking industry recognized the opportunity of this new environment and started setting up branches and subsidiaries in foreign markets. U.S. and European banks were particularly welcome in emerging economies because in many cases a developed banking infrastructure was not in place in these countries, and Western banks were welcomed as a source of expertise. This state of affairs continues to this day, as evidenced by the numbers of expatriate bankers moving from the city of London and Wall Street to banks in the Middle East and Asia. The expansion of Western banks was also facilitated by the development of technology and the use of advanced information technology (IT) infrastructure. For instance, electronic money transference enabled almost instant funding and created a market of interbank liquidity.

During the Clinton administration globalization spread further and deeper as free trade was enhanced by removing many protectionist barriers. Globalization flourished as markets opened up; new capital was made available to do business with Latin America, Asia, and Central and Eastern Europe.[1]

A paradox of this development was that, by opening their borders to free trade with the rest of the world, these countries created potential vulnerabilities. They embraced the free market principle as it gave them a way to get out of isolation and poverty by accepting the money that came from international lenders. However, simultaneously they built up a substantial amount of foreign debt. Governments were not ready to enter what David Smick has called this "ocean of liquidity."[2]

A SERIES OF EMERGING-MARKET CRISES

Free capital flows set the stage for various emerging-market crises such as the Asian currency crisis of 1997–1998. Each crisis was faintly similar: The emerging economy suffered either a full-scale banking crisis or a currency crisis or both. The reasons behind these crises are described most accurately by Frederic Mishkin[3] and Martin Wolf.[4]

First of all, as mentioned earlier, governments were unprepared for the impact of the liberalization of free markets and made clear policy mistakes. Opening up one's borders while one's local banking system is still undeveloped results in a highly leveraged debt buildup as well as a deterioration of loan origination standards. A surfeit of money tends to produce this situation. Many of the loans originated in the local banking systems defaulted. In any situation, as banks start experiencing a rise in bad loans, they increase write-downs and loan loss provisions, and with-draw from lending. This then has a knock-on effect on the economy, and leads to a slowdown in the economic growth process. This is the second phase described in Frederic Mishkin's scenario, the buildup toward a currency crisis. During this phase the government has to step in and come to the rescue. However, for emerging economies their finan-cial strength as a lender of last resort (LOLR) is limited, and often such governments undertake the process with help from the International Monetary Fund (IMF). A drop in public spending is the inevitable result of this process.

Investor confidence (by local residents and foreign investors) disap-pears rapidly at this point, and this triggers the third phase: the currency crisis, once most investors withdraw their money from the country. The central banks of these emerging countries are then faced with a stark choice. Either they have to raise interest rates sharply to support their currency, which will push most people who are in debt into default, or they have to stop intervening and allow their currency to devalue, which will produce inflation and ultimately also cause defaults where much of the borrowed money is in foreign currency. The final phase is the result of the choices to be made in phase three: an unavoidable deep economic recession.

Crises like this have occurred on a regular basis over the past three decades. A study from Hutchison and Neuberger (2002) showed that between 1975 and 1997, 33 bank crises, 51 currency crises, and 20 "twin crises" took place in emerging economies.[5]

A look at the crisis in Thailand in 1997 confirms that events here followed almost exactly the path described by Mishkin. Paul Krugman provides an in-depth analysis of the Asian crisis in his book, which we summarize here.[6]

In the first instance, foreign investors were tending to avoid Latin America after the so-called Tequila Crisis of 1994. This was the series of events in which Mexico suffered a severe currency crisis that year, in part arising from policy mistakes made by President Carlos Salinas de Gortari's government. They focused instead on Asia, and Thailand in particular, which was in the process of converting from an agricultural into an industrial economy. The industrial sector was expanding rapidly, financed by foreign money, to the point where Thailand became an "Asian tiger" with almost double-digit economic growth rates year on year. Foreign banks were feeding this expansion with foreign currencies that were converted immediately into Thai baht (THB), necessary because local entrepreneurs could not use Japanese yen (JPY), U.S. dollars (USD), or German deutsche marks (DEM) to pay workers or buy property.

Due to this increased demand the THB started to appreciate in value. But the Thai central bank wanted to prevent this and keep the THB stable against other currencies. In fact this turned out to be a significant mistake because it stimulated credit growth. In order to keep the THB stable the Thai central bank constantly had to sell its own currency and buy foreign currencies, generally USD. As a result the money supply in THB increased but also the foreign currency reserves of the central bank started rising. A speculative bubble was building up, but instead of halting the support of its own currency the central bank of Thailand (as did all central banks in the region) began to limit the capital inflow. This was done by buying back in the market the THB that they had just sold. In essence the central bank was turning on the money printing press. This acceleration in the money supply, M2, created higher interest rates and rising inflation, which was an incentive for local companies to start borrowing even more in foreign currency, which was much cheaper. The equation[7] $GDP = M2 \times V$ was in full force and the central bank was not wise to the fact that the economy was overheating rapidly.

This development could have been prevented if the currency support had been wound down in time. This did not happen. As inflation rose wages also rose, which lowered productivity and also made exports more expensive. Consequently, exports fell, and a current account deficit was created.

An important element in this lending process was the existence of a middle man between the foreign lender and the local borrower, in the form of a so-called finance company. This was not a local bank but a facilitator that converted the foreign loan into the local currency and determined the interest rate to the borrower. Such firms dominated the lending business. As these finance companies did not operate like a classic bank, where the lending is backed by deposits, they were less disciplined in their loan origination processes. They also expected loan defaults to be covered by the government and ultimately the taxpayer. This moral hazard itself breeds a dangerous complacence, as we explain in a later chapter.

At a certain point, as is the case with all bubbles, investors started losing confidence and withdrew. The borrowing from abroad decreased rapidly and created an additional problem for the central bank. Due to the drop in foreign lending the demand for THB fell. The current account deficit intensified this drop further as imports outpaced exports, which put extra selling pressure on the THB. The central bank had to do the opposite to what it had been doing for a while, meaning buying THB and selling foreign currencies. However, this operation is more difficult than the first one, because while a central bank can print an unlimited amount of its own currency, it certainly cannot do this with foreign currencies.

A policy alternative for the central bank could have been to raise interest rates in order to reduce the money supply, but this was not an easy solution as the economy was struggling and to do this would discourage economic activity still further. It was also too late to withdraw support for the THB as this would trigger a devaluation of the currency, which would have driven many borrowers into insolvency as they had liabilities in a foreign currency. In fact the Thai central bank postponed either decision in the hope that it could buy time, but ultimately this led to a currency crisis and an effective devaluation of the currency in any case.

The Thai story is similar to a number of other emerging-market crises over the past three decades. The common thread for many of them is an artificially low exchange rate for the local currency, which amounts to currency manipulation, and which is not reversed in time to prevent recession. And as many of the economies in the region follow the same policies, the contagion effect of any crisis is high.

The best example of this is what occurred in Argentina at the turn of the century. From the point of view of productivity and exports, Argentina became uncompetitive after its neighbor Brazil decided to devalue its own currency. The Argentinean peso remained pegged against the U.S. dollar, which at that time (only one or two years into its introduction) was strong against the euro. The euro reached a low against the U.S. dollar at around 0.82 and this negatively impacted export opportunities to the eurozone.[8]

The list of countries affected in similar ways is a long one, and includes Mexico, Brazil, Argentina, Thailand, Vietnam, and Indonesia. In every case the cost to the economy was high. Public debt as a percentage of GDP went over 10 percent more than half of the time in these cases, as shown in Figure 1.1. Furthermore the drop in output was also significant, and it took an

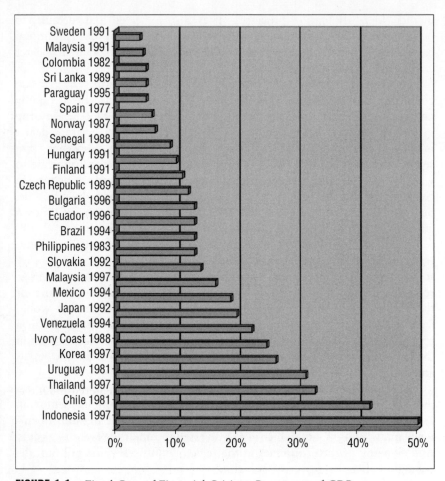

FIGURE 1.1   Fiscal Cost of Financial Crisis as Percentage of GDP
Source: Caprio et al. (2003).[9]

average of over three years for each country to return to positive growth.
This is shown in Table 1.1 and Figure 1.2.

LOW-YIELD ENVIRONMENT DUE TO NEW PLAYERS IN THE FINANCIAL MARKETS

The countries experiencing this sort of crisis learned their lessons and
implemented a more stable export-driven growth model, one in which their

TABLE 1.1 Drop in Output as Percentage of GDP

Country	% of GDP
Japan	48%
Chile	46%
Thailand	40%
Indonesia	39%
Malaysia	33%
Philippines	26%
South Korea	17%

Source: IMF and World Bank.

reserves were immediately converted into U.S. dollars and other foreign currencies such as euros and Swiss francs. So the experience of the currency crises of the 1980s and 1990s were one of the reasons leading to a savings glut in U.S. dollars, and one of the core roots of the crisis we would experience from 2007 onward.

Over time these rising global flows of trade and capital also caused financial imbalances. The U.S. economy started to build up a substantial current-account deficit, as it increased its imports. Developing countries such as China and India liberalized their economies and entered the international scene to participate in this commercial expansion, and after a while Southeast Asian emerging-market economies and oil-exporting countries were funding the U.S. current-account deficit. The United States would act under all this as consumer of last resort, and the current account balance sheets of these countries made a sudden and drastic reverse. This is illustrated in Figures 1.3 and 1.4.

As these Asian and oil-exporting countries were accumulating ever more reserves, a significant new player emerged in the form of the sovereign wealth fund (SWF). SWFs are state-owned investment vehicles which invest their surpluses in global financial assets. Unlike central bank reserves, their portfolio is diversified across a wide range of assets such as equity, real estate, fixed income, hedge funds, and private equity. Together with the hedge funds, Asian central banks and the private equity firms became in effect the new power brokers of the financial markets.[10] By 2006 the SWFs, together with the Asian central banks, became the biggest asset managers in the world, as shown in Figures 1.5 and 1.6.

These new players added new liquidity to the global markets and by 2006 they represented (including the leverage part of hedge funds[11]) roughly

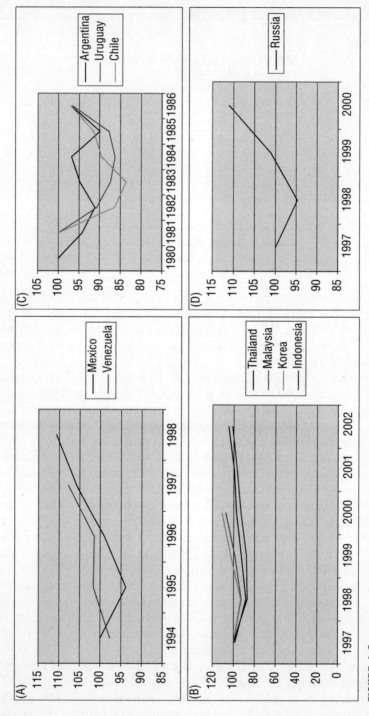

FIGURE 1.2 Loss of GDP During Four Major Emerging-Market Crises
Source: IMF.

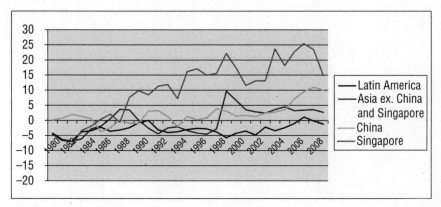

FIGURE 1.3   Evolution of Current Account Balances of Major Emerging-Market Regions, 1980–2008
Source: Institute for International Finance.

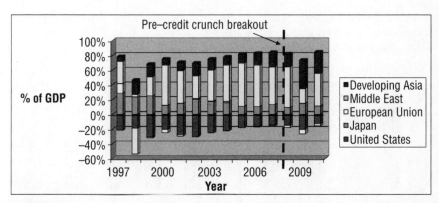

FIGURE 1.4   Development in U.S. Current Accounts Balance as a Percentage of GDP
Source: IMF.

$13.6 trillion. Apart from the Asian central banks, the petrodollar countries were initially investing their reserves in U.S. and European government bonds. This extra liquidity depressed long-term interest rates. According to a McKinsey study, in the U.S. bond market long-term interest rates were pushed down by an estimated 130 basis points.[12]

At first this phenomenon was called an "interest rate conundrum" by the chairman of the U.S. Federal Reserve, Alan Greenspan, in June 2005. The Federal Reserve started raising U.S. interest rates from 2004 onward. However, despite hiking short-term rates aggressively, the long end of the

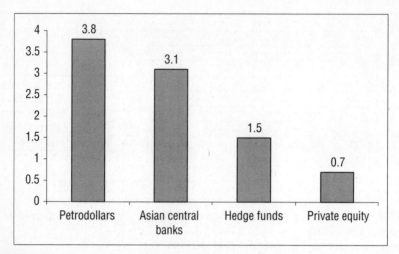

FIGURE 1.5 The New Power Brokers' Assets under Management in $ Trillions (2006)
Note: $1.5 trillion of hedge funds are assets under management. Their real exposure is estimated to be leveraged up to $6 trillion.
Source: McKinsey Global Institute, 2006.

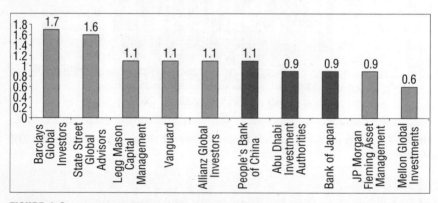

FIGURE 1.6 Top Ten Asset Managers in $ Trillions (2006)
Source: McKinsey Global Institute, 2006.

U.S. Treasury curve continued to drop. This was not limited to the United States but was a worldwide phenomenon. From June 2004 to June 2005 the U.S. central bank raised the Fed funds rate eight times, from 1 percent up to 3 percent. Over that same period the yield on the U.S. Treasury's benchmark 10-year note fell from around 4.8 percent to around 4 percent, as shown in Figure 1.7.

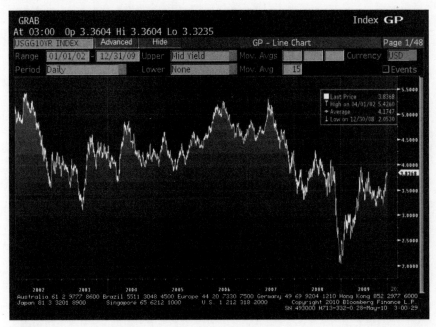

FIGURE 1.7 U.S. 10-year Treasury Note 2000–2009
Source: © Bloomberg Finance L.P. All rights reserved. Used with permission.

At the time, Mr. Greenspan did not believe that this was due to large flows of foreign capital from emerging-market countries running large surpluses against the United States. Of course, now we know that this was indeed the case. As the price of oil almost doubled from 2002 to 2006, the petrodollar exporting countries became one of the most important suppliers of capital, as shown in Figure 1.8.

As the inflow of new money was continuous during this period, this depressed credit spreads and so investors became less risk-averse and extended along the credit curve in their search for yield. Also, among these SWFs and Asian central banks there was a shift in risk appetite. The consequence of all this was something Professor Milton Friedman had predicted along general lines many years before: the danger of too much money chasing too few goods, which creates inflationary assets and fuels an asset price bubble. Private equity was boosted due to excess cheap credit being available. Cheap credit also boosted the hedge fund industry using leverage. Finally, credit spreads were structurally pushed lower due to supply– and demand–driven synthetic CDO structures which were issued on a monthly basis. The Asian and oil-exporting countries' investment

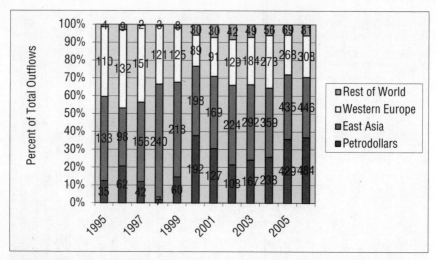

FIGURE 1.8   Net Capital Outflows from Countries with Current Account Surpluses in $ Billions
Source: IMF; McKinsey Global Institute.

policies played an important role in the dynamics of this seemingly prosperous environment.

Greenspan's successor, Chairman Ben Bernanke, came closer to explaining the interest rate conundrum. He referred to it as the savings glut. The United States was acting as a kind of "spender of last resort" by creating a huge current account deficit that was fueling a housing market boom. However, at the time he detected the problem, he downplayed its risks. In 2009, though, the Federal Reserve chairman delivered a *mea culpa*, pinpointing the large capital inflows as a force lifting the U.S. economy, but failing to stop Americans from going on a destructive spending spree.

> *The global imbalances were the joint responsibility of the United States and our trading partners, and although the topic was a perennial one at international conferences, we collectively did not do enough to reduce those imbalances. However, the responsibility to use the resulting capital inflows effectively fell primarily on the receiving countries, particularly the United States.*[13]

Concern over the deficit in the U.S. current account—a broad trade measure that includes investment flows—and its flip side, a massive Chinese surplus, would dominate meetings of the Group of Seven (G7) nations, before a credit crisis and global recession gave policy makers something else to worry about. U.S. officials did not realize that their country being the destination of choice for world lenders was a problem. Mr. Bernanke has said that he now knows otherwise. The flood of cheap (foreign) money fueled a housing boom that ended up being a bubble. As he stated,

> *The risk-management systems of the private sector and government oversight of the financial sector in the United States and some other industrial countries failed to ensure that the inrush of capital was prudently invested.*

As a result, that failure has destroyed investor confidence and frozen credit markets worldwide since the summer of 2007 when the bubble burst. One could compare the position of the United States with that of Latin American or Asian countries during their crises. However, there is one major difference, which is the strength and status of the U.S. dollar. During every emerging-market crisis foreign investors fled out of the local market. In this case, however, it was the contrary. Investors considered U.S. government bonds to be a safe haven, which supported the dollar.

ARTIFICIALLY LOW EXCHANGE RATES

Nevertheless, emerging-market crises only partially describe this savings glut. Martin Wolf describes this accurately in his book.[14] It is the result of a mix of policy decisions and private behavior. The decision from emerging-market countries to run current account surpluses and reinvest their savings mainly in U.S. dollar assets is a clear policy decision. This is done via exchange rate protectionism, by keeping their local currencies artificially undervalued against their major trading partners. As we noted, this decision was partly inspired by the experience in these countries during previous crises. The rise in demand for oil and consequently the higher oil price gave the Middle Eastern countries a boost in savings which were not reinvested in their own country but repatriated to the United States. This is a pure policy intervention.

Then there was the aftermath of the dot-com bubble, where investors but also companies in the developed world became much more cautious in their investment decisions, which increased the saving rate as well. This is a behavioral response.

Last but not least, there was a shift of income from labor to capital, especially in Europe and Japan, which was not offset by an increase in investments, which automatically raised the saving surplus. As far as Europe and Japan are concerned, this shift is also mainly driven by demographics. Typically, in an aging society there is less need for investments. Here the balance flips more toward behavioral reactions than a policy response.

RECOMMENDATIONS AND SOLUTIONS FOR GLOBAL IMBALANCES

In this chapter we highlighted the problems created by global currency reserve imbalances, created in turn by current account surpluses in emerging countries, which were a result of lessons learned from previous emerging-market crises. As a result of policy, emerging-market countries kept their currencies artificially low via systematic intervention in the currency market. The ultimate goal was and is to prevent (speculative) capital flowing into the country. This strategy created, and still creates, excess foreign exchange reserves which are reinvested abroad, predominantly in the United States.

At the time of this writing, these imbalances were still in place. One of the main challenges for policy makers will be to convince these emerging economies to boost their internal demand instead of repatriating all their savings to the West. Figure 1.9 highlights where the problems are located.

Figure 1.9 also shows the worrisome situation for a country like the United States where one-third of its investments are funded from abroad. This makes it highly dependent on such flows. This is not a problem as long as the U.S. retains its status as a top-quality borrower. But in situations where the U.S. public debt is reaching astronomical levels, as a result of the bailouts of the banking sector and other economic stimulus packages, this might become an issue.

On April 1, 2009, the G7 and G20 met in London to take joint measures against the crisis. During that meeting world leaders addressed only briefly the global imbalances that were created over time. Unfortunately, the discussion was focused on the wrong parameters. The debate centered around the question of whether there was a need to replace the U.S. dollar as a reserve currency. Not surprisingly, China was the leading voice in this debate, as the country held in December 2009 approximately 24.30 percent of U.S. Treasuries, or USD 894.8 billion in nominal value.

However, this is diverting attention from the real problem. The focus should be on reducing these current account surpluses, and that of China in particular as it has the largest reserves of all emerging markets and it is still growing. This is easier said than done, as at this moment the U.S.

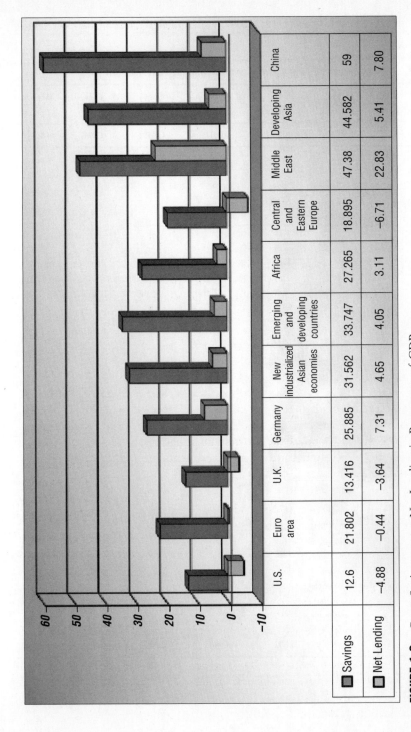

	U.S.	Euro area	U.K.	Germany	New industrialized Asian economies	Emerging and developing countries	Africa	Central and Eastern Europe	Middle East	Developing Asia	China
Savings	12.6	21.802	13.416	25.885	31.562	33.747	27.265	18.895	47.38	44.582	59
Net Lending	−4.88	−0.44	−3.64	7.31	4.65	4.05	3.11	−6.71	22.83	5.41	7.80

FIGURE 1.9 Gross Savings versus Net Lending in Percentage of GDP

Source: IMF, *World Economic Outlook*, October 2008.

TABLE 1.2 Overview of MENA Currency and Interest Rate Market

	Saudi Arabia	Kuwaiti Dinar	UAE Dirham	Bahraini Dinar	Qatari Rial	Omani Rial	Moroccan Dirham
	SAR	KWD	AED	BHD	QAR	OMR	MAD
Fully convertible	Yes	Yes	Yes	Yes	Yes	Yes	No
Liquid FWD	Yes Up to 2 years	Yes Up to 2 years	Yes Up to 2 years Only commercial	Yes Up to 1 year Only commercial	No Up to 6 months Only commercial	No No	No No
Longer FWDS	Upon request	Upon request	Upon request	Upon request	Upon request	No	No
Options	No	No	No	No	No	No	No
IRS	Up to 2 years	No	No	No	No	No	No
Fra's	Up to 2 years	No	No	No	No	No	No
Offshore deposit lending	Yes	Yes	No due to withholding tax	No	Yes	No	10% tax on local deposits
Pegged at	3.75	Pegged to the USD against an undisclosed basket of currencies. Current midpoint 0.27200	1$/3.6725 AED	0.376	1$/3.64 QAR	1$/0.3845 OMR	Basket
Since	1986	20/05/2007	2002	1980	1980	1986	1980

Algerian Dinar	Tunisian Dinar	Egyptian Pound	Jordanian Dinar	Lebanese Pound	Libyan Dinar	Syrian Pound
DZD	TND	EGP	JOD	LBP	LYD	SYP
No Buy spot only Sell on firm order only	Yes	Yes	Yes 0.1% commission Buying $	No	No Cash market In Tunis	No
No No	No Up to 9–12 months	Reasonably Only commercial L/C reference	No Only commercial	No No	No No Only commercial Case by case	No No
No	Upon request	Upon request	Upon request	No	No	No
No	No	No	No	No	No	No
No	No	No	No	No	No	No
No	No	No	No	No	No	No
No	10% tax on local deposits	No	No	No	No	No
1$/72.647 DZD	Managed floating	Free floating	Basket	1$/1,507.50 LBP	1$/1.3108 LYD	To the EUR daily
1980	1980	1980	1982	1980	1985	14/02/2006

government will need the rest of the world more than ever with a runaway public deficit of over $3 trillion just for the fiscal year 2009. And the fiscal cost of reducing the debt of the credit bubble will be higher in the years ahead.

Any abrupt change in policy would lead to a sudden collapse of the U.S. dollar and a rapid rise in interest rates. These are two things that the Chinese government, as a large investor in U.S. dollar assets, would want to avoid as the mark-to-market of its USD bond portfolio would be heavily and negatively affected. But a first step in the right direction would be reducing the pace of the current account surplus rise. Wolf (2009) calculated that by 2012 the current account surplus could grow from USD 449 billion at the end of 2008 to USD 700 billion. Simultaneously, China's foreign exchange reserves could almost double to USD 4 trillion. We draw similar conclusions to those of Wolf.[15]

The only way to slow this rapid rise is by stimulating internal demand. A rise in internal demand should come from both the private and public sectors. The latter is already taking place as the Chinese government increased spending in order to deal with the fallout of the global recession. In fact, the first signs of economic recovery across the globe during 2009 were related to the increase in Chinese public spending. In order to improve private demand, special attention should be paid from the government toward education and a basic health care system.

Then ideally taxes would be raised on Chinese companies as they show a high savings rate. A rise in corporate taxes would help the development of the corporate bond market to finance part of their investments and simultaneously force these companies into more discipline. This in turn would improve the condition of the loan portfolios of the local banks. The extra income from these taxes could be used to create a so-called Silver Fund, which could serve as a pension fund to deal with the aging of their population.

A next vital step would be to revalue the Chinese currency against the U.S. dollar (USD). Although a de-pegging of the yuan was announced in June 2010, the currency is still a long way from being free floating. The latter is something that should be promoted among all emerging-market countries whose currencies are still pegged to the USD.

Currency revaluation would go hand in hand with general financial reforms such as the opening up of financial markets and free entry of foreign direct investments into the country. As mentioned earlier with respect to China, emerging markets need to develop an in-depth bond market in their local currency with long maturities. Bond markets in domestic emerging markets have expanded, but the maturities are still short. For example, most of the maturities in the emerging-market bonds are issued at between three and five years. There are longer maturities available but these are generally illiquid.

As an example, Table 1.2 gives an overview of the limitations in the Middle Eastern and North African (MENA) currency and interest rate markets. The situation is not any better in the Chinese currency and bond market. The Chinese renminbi, for example, is still nonconvertible and hedges need to be made by foreign companies via the nondeliverable forward market.

Of course, certain conditions need to be fulfilled to establish a more robust financial infrastructure.

First, the governments of these countries need to build up credibility among their own citizens in order to convince them to start investing in their country's own debt. Fiscal discipline will be an important factor. Furthermore, the establishment of a legal platform is needed where respect toward property rights is guaranteed. Also, there needs to be secure bankruptcy legislation structure in place, and the installment of independent regulators. The regulator must ensure strict guidelines regarding deposit guarantees in case of bank runs.

Second, it is important to give foreign investors free access to their markets.

Third, special focus should go toward the establishment of a pension fund and insurance industry. These will automatically be important participants in the growing local bond market. This does not necessarily mean that they have to buy all the domestic debt, but they will give added value toward stability and create a base for long-term investors that tries to match long-term assets versus long-term liabilities. When this financial infrastructure is in place and has become less fragile, a final step can be made to make the local currency fully floating. This will enable banks and companies to lend and borrow in the local currency and reduce currency mismatches.

As with the bank regulation proposals that we state elsewhere in this book, the preceding recommendations will not guarantee a crisis-free global economy. Crises are inherent to the capitalistic system, but of course what is important is that the markets work to mitigate their impact.

CHAPTER 2

The Rise of Derivatives and Systemic Risk

Hand in hand, and partly connected, with the development of globalization was an exponential increase in the use of financial derivative contracts. The rise in worldwide commercial trade also increased the hedging requirements of corporations, and they started using derivatives as the appropriate tool to fulfill these needs. However, use of derivatives was not restricted to companies and their commercial purposes. The hedge fund industry grew in size from the 1990s onward and became one of the new *power brokers* of the financial markets. This term was used for the first time in a report from McKinsey in October 2007.[1] Together with the sovereign wealth funds, Asian central banks, and private equity firms, hedge funds played a dominant role in the globalization of the financial markets.

These four players added extra liquidity to the market and by 2006 they represented approximately $13.6 trillion of assets under management. In the case of the hedge fund industry, the participants worked on a leveraged basis. McKinsey calculated that on average the leverage factor of the hedge fund industry was around four times the assets under management. Figure 1.5 in chapter 1 showed the size of the respective market participants by the end of 2006. However, accounting for the average leverage used by hedge funds, they became the most important player in the market with $6 trillion of trading assets.

The sheer volume of growth of these assets exerted downward pressure on the yield curve, a phenomenon that Federal Reserve Chairman Alan Greenspan thought represented an "interest rate conundrum" at the time. But the most important aspect of this development was the rise in the use of derivatives in the markets.[2] Hedge fund firms were the major users of these financial instruments, partly because of their higher ease of market entry and also because they allowed the possibility of putting on more complex trades.

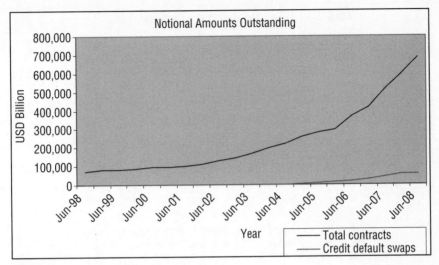

FIGURE 2.1 Growth of Derivatives Use
Source: BIS, http://www.bis.org/.

Figure 2.1, using data reported by the Bank for International Settlements (BIS), shows the exponential rise in volume of these financial instruments.

By the end of June 2008, according to the BIS, the notional amounts outstanding of over-the-counter (OTC) contracts stood at $683 trillion. Interest rate derivatives are still the most important derivative tool with $458 trillion among OTC derivatives. However, other derivative instruments have also seen high growth. Together with the expansion of the *shadow banking* system and the intense use of securitization techniques, credit default swaps (CDSs) have been used in ever larger volumes. In 2006 the total outstanding notional amount of CDS trades was $20.3 trillion, but by the end of June 2008 it had more than doubled to $57.3 trillion. Table 2.1 gives the rundown of the volume in each underlying asset class in the OTC derivatives market in the first half of 2008. Following the financial crash of 2007–2009, this volume started to decline for the first time since the BIS started monitoring this number. However, CDS use declined only 1 percent, compared to an average six-month growth rate over the past three years of 45 percent.

SYSTEMIC RISK

The exponential increase in use of derivatives resulted in increased fears of systemic risk in the system. We define *systemic risk* here to mean risk of a

TABLE 2.1   The Global OTC Derivatives Market, 2008

Type	Amount USD Billion
Forex	62,983
Interest rates	458,304
Equity	10,177
Commodities	13,229
Credit default swaps	57,325
Unallocated	81,708
Total	683,726

Note: Includes foreign exchange, interest rate, equity, commodity, and credit derivatives of nonreporting institutions, based on the latest Triennial Central Bank Survey of Foreign Exchange and Derivatives Market Activity.
Source: BIS, June 2008.

chain reaction of financial failures, the end result of which is the dislocation and failure of the global banking system.

The first indication of this risk was in 1998 when the hedge fund Long Term Capital Management (LTCM) collapsed after the failure of highly leveraged positions that it had built up. Between 1994, the year the fund was founded, and September 1998, it put on a derivative position of approximately $1.25 trillion (notional value of outstanding derivatives), with only $130 billion of assets under management. The Asian crisis in 1997, and the Russian crisis the following year, resulted in significant losses on the fund's trading books, which triggered a snowball effect due to higher margin calls that the fund was obliged to fulfill. The abrupt unwinding of the positions threatened to destabilize financial markets in such a way that the U.S. Federal Reserve decided it had to intervene and bail out the hedge fund. If the Fed had not done so, the domino effect of counterparty banks failing would most probably have resulted in a collapse of the financial system in September 1998. The total price of the bailout at that time was $3.6 billion.

This amount would be only a fraction of the total damage that would be caused 10 years later. On September 15, 2008, the bankruptcy of U.S. investment bank Lehman Brothers triggered a dislocation of financial markets that went far beyond the LTCM debacle. The estimated loss in market capitalization in the global equity market alone for the month of October of that year exceeded $10 trillion.

The true cost of the collapse of Lehman's is at present difficult to quantify, but taking into account all the bailouts, nationalizations, and rescue packages that governments across the globe had to implement in order to keep the global economy afloat, the number is close to the amount that was lost on global stock markets between October 2008 and March 2009.

Possibly at the time, but most definitely in hindsight, the U.S. government's failure to rescue Lehman Brothers was the biggest policy mistake of the entire financial crisis. What happened after September 15, 2008, had in fact been accurately predicted by the late economist and Nobel Prize winner Hyman Minsky. Because of the interconnection of financial markets, counterparties of Lehman Brothers were forced to sell out of their positions in order to acquire the necessary funds or liquidity. This sudden selling pressure led in turn to a further decline in asset values, which triggered a collapse in market prices and liquidity.[3] This is known in the literature as a *Minsky moment*.

Brunnermeier (2009) provides a good description of this event. A quotation from this reference is as follows:

> *For example, investment bank A is entering into a derivative transaction with one of its clients. Simultaneously, investment bank A hedges itself in the interbank market with investment bank B, which has an interest to take on the risk. In this situation all parties are 100 percent hedged and via the ISDAs they have with each other they can net out and neutralize the risks among each other. The problem is though that investment bank A is not aware of the positions investment bank B has. This is a similar situation to what happened at the time of LTCM. UBS, Merrill and Goldman Sachs to name a few had no idea they were exposed indirectly to each other. If both investment banks A and B, shown in the diagram [Figure 2.2], do not want their clients to offset the outstanding positions via netting, then these clients will have the choice between either giving extra collateral, or buying a hedge via credit default swaps because of the counterparty credit risk.*
>
> *This scenario unfolded weeks after Lehman's bankruptcy, back in September 2008. Every single bank got panicked that their counterparties would go under, and they all started to hedge against each other in the CDS market. This is the reason why spreads of credit default swaps exploded in the aftermath of Lehman Brothers' collapse.[4]*

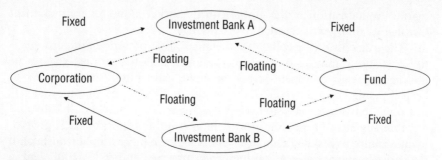

FIGURE 2.2   A Network of Interest Rate Swap Arrangements

FIGURE 2.3   Behavior of VIX Contract During Period 2006–2009
Source: © Bloomberg Finance L.P. All rights reserved. Used with permission. Visit
www.bloomberg.com.

Figure 2.2 is an illustration of the network of interest rate swap arrangements that Brunnermeier refers to. Figure 2.3 shows the price of the CBOE
Volatility Index (VIX) contract during the time of the crisis, the period
2006–2009.

The interconnections in the derivatives market and the risks they
represented reignited the debate on curtailing the use of the instruments,

or at least centralizing them through a clearing exchange. In 2003 the investor Warren Buffett had called such products "financial weapons of mass destruction." This is an unfortunate and misleading description. However it highlights the very real nature of systemic risk in the market. In his Berkshire Hathaway newsletter of that year, Buffett argues:

> . . . the macro picture is dangerous and getting more so. Large amounts of risk, particularly credit risk, have become concentrated in the hands of relatively few derivatives dealers, who in addition trade extensively with one other. The troubles of one could quickly infect the others. On top of that, these dealers are owed huge amounts by nondealer counterparties. Some of these counterparties, as I've mentioned, are linked in ways that could cause them to contemporaneously run into a problem because of a single event (such as the implosion of the telecom industry or the precipitous decline in the value of merchant power projects). Linkage, when it suddenly surfaces, can trigger serious systemic problems.[5]

Certainly one cannot downplay the dangers of systemic risk. Table 2.2 suggests that systemic risk is a potential great concern. In 2008 in the United States almost 97 percent of all outstanding OTC derivatives was concentrated on the books of only five U.S. banks. Almost 50 percent was on the books of just one counterparty, JPMorgan Chase Bank.

Derivatives had previously been in the headlines because of losses, misuse, fraud, and so on. During the 1990s there were events such as one in Orange County, California, where use of interest rate swaps had caused the bankruptcy of the Californian municipality. Then there was the failure from large losses of the British bank Barings in 1995. At the beginning of the twenty-first century the Enron failure occurred, in which fraud and the use of derivatives were prevalent. However, in these examples it was more misconduct and a breach of internal risk guidelines that was the cause of huge losses. The instrument itself was not really to blame.

After the Lehman collapse derivatives came under renewed attack as one of the causes of the financial turmoil. Both in Europe and the United States there is a growing consensus among politicians that derivatives were the cause of financial failure. However this is an intellectually dishonest and demagogic debate. As we show in this book, derivatives did not cause the crash. Their role was more akin to that of the piano player in the orchestra. There is nothing inherently wrong with a derivative as a financial product. The bigger problem is the leverage that usually surrounds the instrument. Whether it was LTCM, Orange County, the Latin American

TABLE 2.2 Concentration Risk of OTC Derivatives among U.S. Banks

Rank	Bank Name	State	Total Assets	Total Derivatives	Total Futures (Exch Tr)
1	JPMorgan Chase Bank N.A.	OH	$1,768,657	$87,688,008	$1,442,086
2	Bank of America N.A.	NC	1,359,071	38,673,967	1,622,080
3	Citibank N.A.	NV	1,207,007	35,645,429	253,586
4	Wachovia Bank N.A.	NC	664,223	4,221,834	223,423
5	HSBC Bank USA N.A.	DE	181,587	4,133,712	85,293
6	Wells Fargo Bank N.A.	SD	514,853	1,429,088	174,358
7	Bank of New York Mellon	NY	218,699	1,193,652	28,549
8	State Street Bank & Trust Co.	MA	276,291	869,294	2,054
9	SunTrust Bank	GA	170,007	276,689	63,232
10	PNC Bank N.A.	PA	134,780	198,478	26,441
11	Northern Trust Co.	IL	68,930	175,128	0
12	Keybank N.A.	OH	97,811	136,302	20,652
13	National City Bank	OH	141,501	123,530	16,007
14	U.S. Bank N.A.	OH	242,597	97,056	1,640
15	Merrill Lynch Bank USA	UT	61,643	94,255	72,285
16	Regions Bank	AL	139,556	80,094	13,964
17	Branch Banking and Trust Co.	NC	133,166	71,044	3,599
18	RBS Citizens N.A.	RI	132,609	59,474	0
19	Fifth Third Bank	OH	67,318	58,101	94
20	LaSalle Bank N.A.	IL	63,388	33,701	0
21	Union Bank of California N.A.	CA	62,431	33,557	2,361
22	UBS Bank USA	UT	26,176	33,317	0
23	Deutsche Bank TR Co.	NY	43,932	27,004	0
24	Morgan Stanley Bank N.A.	UT	37,638	25,941	0
25	First Tennessee Bank N.A.	TN	32,587	24,546	287
Top 25 commercial banks and trust companies with derivatives			$7,846,461	$175,403,202	$4,051,991
Other commercial banks and trust companies with derivatives			2,703,969	438,563	6,816
Total commercial banks and trust companies with derivatives			10,550,430	175,841,765	4,058,807

Source: Comptroller of the Currency (OCC), third quarter 2008.

Total Options (Exch Tr)	Total Forwards (OTC)	Total Swaps (OTC)	Total Options (OTC)	Total Credit Derivatives (OTC)	Spot FX
$2,349,629	$8,949,110	$54,385,247	$11,384,205	$9,177,731	$218,733
643,185	3,651,347	26,796,894	3,479,789	2,480,672	237,758
432,226	5,071,607	20,210,646	6,737,581	2,939,783	536,543
87,961	211,515	2,913,470	464,389	321,076	15,248
113,974	565,779	1,938,203	277,515	1,152,948	76,457
21,694	468,891	562,659	199,766	1,720	19,149
58,355	383,966	384,724	336,641	1,417	56,668
713	786,206	17,927	57,249	5,145	54,802
26,671	14,275	137,461	31,987	3,063	407
12,500	6,079	124,859	23,660	4,940	1,580
0	165,238	9,232	389	269	22,761
4,400	15,325	79,430	8,805	7,690	1,277
350	12,326	49,853	42,700	2,293	123
9,000	23,871	51,272	9,618	1,655	878
246	614	12,086	0	9,025	0
3,500	1,222	59,482	1,487	439	7
0	8,632	49,228	9,533	52	57
0	4,890	53,129	1,228	228	37
0	8,999	39,367	9,333	308	863
0	0	24,414	7,398	1,890	0
0	4,371	18,303	8,522	0	1,059
0	0	33,317	0	0	0
0	391	20,941	601	5,071	0
0	0	2,156	0	23,785	0
0	10,780	11,200	2,189	0	2
$3,764,404	$20,365,524	$107,985,498	$23,094,585	$16,141,200	$1,244,408
2,869	58,678	290,590	72,421	7,188	1,523
3,767,404	20,424,203	108,276,088	23,167,006	16,148,388	1,245,931

crisis, the 1997 Asian crisis, the 1998 Russian crisis, the dot-com bubble, or the latest bank crash, at the end of the day it was the leverage behind the positions that caused the market disruption.

In the next section we provide recommendations on how to prevent the use of derivatives from creating systemic risk, and how to ensure greater transparency.

DERIVATIVE MARKET SYSTEMIC RISK: SOLUTIONS FOR IMPROVEMENT

Table 2.2 illustrated the seriousness of the systemic risk problem in the banking system. The situation has not improved following the Lehman collapse.

At the time of this writing, President Obama had announced a preliminary plan to regulate financial markets. One of the major points of this Regulatory Reform Plan is to appoint the Federal Reserve Bank as the ultimate systemic risk regulator. In its mandate as ultimate regulator the Fed would have day-to-day supervision of the largest banks. It would also have supervision over nonbank financial companies (such as hedge funds) that reach a size and complexity comparable to (large) banks. The Fed is also likely to be given authority over bank capital requirements, including an extra buffer rule for financial institutions with a high systemic profile (for example, JPMorgan Chase, as shown in Table 2.2).

This is a considerable breadth of power to be vested in one institution. The Federal Reserve is viewed with much credibility and respect in the international financial markets, as a nonpoliticized and independent institution. These added powers may undermine this credibility if the Fed carries out a less than perfect job. Furthermore, directly intervening in the daily management of banks and hedge funds may be impractical and onerous.

As the legislation has not been finalized, it is possible that ultimately only a fraction of the initial proposal will be passed. As it currently stands, the Regulatory Reform Plan reflects the emotions and political rhetoric that were inevitable as a result of the social cost of the crash. As we pointed out earlier, much public opinion holds that derivatives were the major cause of the crisis and so should be banned. However, this is certainly not the solution to the problem.

In response to the Regulatory Reform Plan, a group of international banks formulated suggestions to global regulators and legislators.[6] In a letter to the president of the Federal Reserve Bank of New York,[7] the senior management of the respective banks provided an outline of the initiatives they were planning to take to address systemic risk. To quote from the letter directly, these initiatives included:

- *Implementing data repositories for non-cleared transactions in these markets to ensure appropriate transparency and disclosure, and to assist global supervisors with oversight and surveillance activities.*
- *Clearing for OTC standardized derivative products in these markets.*
- *Enabling customer access to clearing through either direct access as a clearing member or via indirect access, including the benefits of initial margin segregation and position portability.*
- *Delivering robust collateral and margining processes, including portfolio reconciliations, metrics on position and market value breaks, and improved dispute resolution mechanics.*
- *Updating industry governance to be more inclusive of buy-side participants.*
- *Continuing to drive improvement in industry infrastructure as well as to engage and partner with supervisors, globally, to expand upon the substantial improvements that have developed since 2005.*[8]

As far as the clearing procedure is concerned, the banks intend to improve the transparency among credit default swaps (CDSs), interest rate derivatives, and equity derivatives that are traded through them and not cleared through a central clearing party (CCP) to be registered universally in a trade repository. Additionally, they will broaden the number of products with the CCPs that they are already doing business with. On the list are single-name CDSs and overnight index swaps (OISs). The deadline for implementation is the end of 2010. By 2011 the banks intend to add tranched CDS structures to the clearing platform. Furthermore, they are pushing for buy-side customers to have access to a CDS clearing platform as well. In the central platform the collateral of all OTC transactions will be checked electronically on a daily basis.

The group of banks also realized that issues such as limiting the confirmation time of a transaction, increasing the possibility of electronic processing of a deal, and standardizing the documentation of confirmed deals need to be addressed. In the CDS market these are significant problems. For a $57 trillion market, it is a surprising fact that until recently a major share of transactions were submitted manually on a piece of paper, and that the confirmation itself might take weeks and, in some instances, months.

Increasing Transparency via a Global Centralized Clearinghouse

All these initiatives are steps in the right direction and should contribute to the reduction of systemic risk. Certainly the ambition to have tranched structures to be cleared in the near future will prevent situations where the market has to guess who carries which kind of risk. Nevertheless, the initiatives are still limited to the larger banks and remain voluntary for the buy side. If one really wants to know where the risks are located at all times, one should make the participation in the clearing process compulsory for the buy side.

Ultimately, however, a complete solution is yet to be implemented; the clearing landscape still remains decentralized. There are a number of clearing houses that offer a variety of services. There is also a potential conflict of interest as large banks, such as J.P. Morgan and Goldman Sachs, are on the board of the clearing houses. The only robust and complete solution is for the market to implement a robust, unified, global clearing platform.

A major step forward would be having a single clearing party to cover every OTC transaction in the world. The first hurdle to setting this up is a political one: the debate over which jurisdiction should take on that responsibility. One candidate would be the U.S. Federal Reserve, but we can imagine that there would be political resistance from other nations. Therefore, the ideal solution would be a neutral institution such as the United Nations. However, the UN is not organized to undertake this function. The World Bank and the International Monetary Fund (IMF) are possibilities, but they also do not have the proper infrastructure.

The one institution that fits perfectly is the Bank for International Settlements (BIS). The BIS can be considered the diplomatic platform of all the central banks in the world. Senior officials of central banks meet in Basel, Switzerland, on a regular basis to discuss topics such as monetary policy, surveillance of the financial markets, and other governance issues. The BIS already collects data on economics and finance, including data on the OTC derivatives market. In this respect it is logical for the BIS to be the entity where the universal trade depositary should reside.

The BIS also offers several services to central banks. In the foreign exchange market it executes foreign exchange (FX) and gold transactions on behalf of clients; it also provides standard services such as sight/notice accounts and fixed-term deposits. Other products include asset management services in sovereign securities and high-grade assets, and lending services

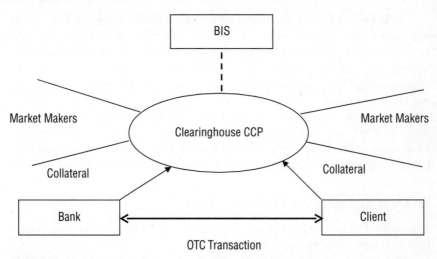

FIGURE 2.4 Recommended Clearinghouse Approach (via BIS)

to other central banks on a collateralized basis.[9] In this respect the BIS already possesses the infrastructure to support the provision of a global clearer of the OTC derivatives market. Our recommended structure is shown in Figure 2.4.

In this clearing process system, the client would enter into a derivative transaction, such as an FX-equity-interest rate derivative or CDS, and would be facing the counterparty bank indirectly via the CCP, which is supervised by the BIS. The BIS would have dealing lines with all market makers in the world that quote derivatives. The dealers would deposit cash as collateral with the BIS. It goes without saying that the CCP must have a AAA-rated government-backed profile. The BIS is such an organization.

Anytime a specific derivative transaction was off-side (i.e., its mark-to-market was negative), the respective counterparty would receive a margin call by the CCP and be required to deposit further collateral. If the request was not respected the position would be closed. This is the same principle used with a margin trading account at a broker.

There is one obstacle. Small-cap corporate clients use derivatives routinely to hedge their commercial risk exposure. However, they do not have the cash to put up as collateral as most of them need structural funding. Closing the possibility to use hedging would have catastrophic consequences to the global economy. (Incidentally, this argument already proves the necessity of derivatives to global economic growth.)

To keep track of all the outstanding transactions, the bank that closes a derivative transaction with such a small-cap client would report it in a central database. This is the registration in a trade depositary that the banks referred to in their letter to the Fed of New York. It would not make any sense to oblige hedge funds to take part in this clearing process while allowing big multinational corporations to stay out of it. Corporations such as Shell, Procter & Gamble, Ikea, Dow Chemical, and so on are big derivative players. They are not different from the hedge funds in this respect. Therefore, at a certain size level we recommend that every market participant, irrespective of their type, must take part in the CCP process.

Leverage and an Expanded Product Range

Even with a global CCP in place, derivatives may suffer from a bad reputation as instruments of mass destruction.

Perhaps education is the answer. Derivatives contributed to substantial savings at corporations because they enabled them to manage their interest-rate risk, commodity risk, and other risks. Therefore, to a certain extent they should be considered an insurance instrument, where one pays a premium for protection against something that might happen in the future that would damage one's interests. If that happened, one would then be compensated. And, as described earlier, such insurance can be used for the proper reasons but from time to time it can also be abused.

To use an analogy, a Ferrari is a beautiful car that, apart from its beautiful design, is associated with speed. In the hands of the wrong person this can be a dangerous tool as well. But should Ferraris be banned?

Often it is the leverage that surrounds derivatives that causes the problem. Investors turn to leverage when their returns are under pressure, and even more so in an environment of low yield and/or low volatility. This was also the major drive during the period that Alan Greenspan identified as an interest rate conundrum. This use of leverage in such a case is almost inherent in a competitive environment. But it is not necessary to ban competition.

After 2001, financial markets got into a period of low volatility. Figure 2.5 illustrates the volatility on the S&P 500 as measured by the VIX Index, which trades on the Chicago Board Options Exchange.

The problem is that this low-volatility environment gives a false sense of safety as it is based upon historical records, and investors have the tendency to make future projections on the back of this. This gives investors (a false) justification to add more leverage to their positions.

Myron Scholes gave a good analogy for this false sense of safety. He compared it with a pack of cars, each driving at 100 miles an hour on the

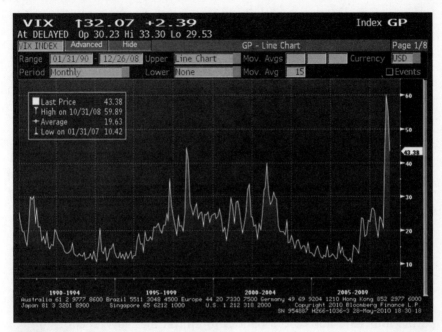

FIGURE 2.5   VIX Index level 1990–2008
Source: © Bloomberg Finance L.P. All rights reserved. Used with permission. Visit www.bloomberg.com.

highway. Every driver involved will not have the feeling he is going fast. However, if one of them has to stop, the braking will probably cause accidents among them all.[10]

This is the reason why governments impose speed limits. What speed means to traffic, leverage means to derivatives, and therefore it is necessary to issue regulation on the use of leverage.

Many of the people involved in the mortgage market were typical families who wanted to buy, for example, a weekend/vacation house in upstate New York or somewhere in Florida or California. None of them, however, could hedge their exposure the way large institutions can. The only thing they could do was to assume house prices would always rise.

Here derivatives could be a valuable tool for households to protect themselves against a drop in property prices. If someone decided to buy a house for $500,000, wouldn't it give some relief to both parties involved in the deal (i.e., the mortgage lender and the homeowner) to know that in case the value of the underlying property were to drop, some kind of protection was built in?

The type of product we are referring to is a *property derivative*. This is a derivative where the underlying asset is a real estate property. The problem with property is that it is something that should be looked at on a case-by-case basis. Because a person's perception of the value of his house can be a rather personal matter, a regional house price index should be used as a reference. This will not give an exact value of a property, but it will give some very good guidance. The index would serve as a proxy hedge, but as we have seen in the current housing crisis, when the value of a house starts to decline, the value of the properties in the surrounding neighborhood follow. In this case, if the house prices in an area were to drop, the derivative put in place would increase in value and offset the loss. Lenders could also use this tool as it would protect them against foreclosures. The premium that is supposed to be paid for this option could be embedded in the mortgage. Instead of paying the total premium up front, one could spread it out over the duration of the loan.

Robert Shiller has referred to the possibility of making the housing market more liquid. Just as the liquidity in the stock market increased over time due to the development of a mature derivative market that attracted more buyers and sellers, it would certainly benefit the housing market where participants have not a lot of options to protect their investments.

Shiller offered a solution to this issue by developing the Case-Shiller U.S. Home Price Index. This is an index that represents the U.S. housing market and can be traded on the Chicago Mercantile Exchange. The problem is, however, that until now this index has been used for speculative purposes. This plays into the hand of critics who doubt the benefits of derivatives and whether they can help the housing market become more liquid.

By contrast, we feel that this criticism is based on fear of the unknown. One can compare this with the way people were skeptical in a previous era when financers started accepting a house or land as collateral in return for advancing a loan. At that time some commentators viewed this activity as a form of magic when a banker started turning land into cash. But this was a major breakthrough for Western society, as Hernando de Soto has concluded.[11] The only way this process could be a success was by having in place a sound legal framework—that is, respect for property rights. The same form of respect is needed for derivatives.

To return to our road traffic analogy, despite the daily number of accidents no one has ever suggested that governments ban cars. Instead, governments continuously work on traffic rules and regulations designed to make cars and driving safer. This is precisely how derivatives should be approached as well.

CHAPTER 3

The Too-Big-to-Fail Bank, Moral Hazard, and Macroprudential Regulation

his chapter is closely related to the previous one on systemic risk in the derivatives market. It describes the risk issues associated with the banking system, as well as the moral hazard created when failing banks are saved. It also discusses how this risk can be mitigated and controlled, and recommends policy for regulators engaged in macroprudential supervision.

The buildup of systemic risk creates a situation where the financial system as a whole comes under threat and the collapse of one bank could potentially trigger the implosion of the entire system. Terms such as *too big to fail* (TBTF), *lender of last resort* (LOLR), and *moral hazard* are closely related. They all serve the purpose of safeguarding the public's deposit money in the event that a financial institution fails. Should this occur, the government, or more specifically the central bank, would usually come to the rescue as an LOLR, because the failure of a bank is likely to have a destabilizing effect on other financial institutions. Contagion effects are closely related to systemic risk. The protection of such a bank renders it TBTF for the system.

BANKS AND MORAL HAZARD

The reason banks get into difficulties will have its origin in a number of factors, including poor risk management and inefficient senior management, but in essence it is because of excessive risk taking. Too much risk can arise because of poor liquidity management, lax loan origination lending standards, uncontrolled trading risks, or even fraud. This excessive risk taking is stimulated via creditors and shareholders having an expectation, however implicit and informal, that ultimately the government will offer a safety net to cover the bank's liabilities should it be on the verge of failing. This is the *moral hazard* risk.

This phenomenon is not limited to the banking sector. The term itself originates in the insurance industry. The fire insurance industry noticed an increase in claims from homeowners who were fully insured and whose properties, by coincidence, had burned down. This often happened when the value of the property was lower than the value of the insurance cover.

In the financial industry the government and the central banks play a pivotal role in maintaining moral hazard. By definition, a central bank that places itself as an LOLR creates a dual principle. First it gives a strong signal to deposit holders not to withdraw their money from the bank, because the central bank is placing resources at the disposal of private banks to keep the credit process going. However, following on from this, it encourages deposit holders to place their money at the bank offering the highest deposit interest rate.

Banks themselves will compete in attracting deposits. The bank that is able to pay the highest deposit rate will attract the most deposits. This can only be realized by taking on more risk. In essence this was what happened with the UK bank Northern Rock. Deposit holders had assumed that the Bank of England would bail out the bank in case of difficulties. Due to its more aggressive credit portfolio, Northern Rock was able to pay out a higher rate on its clients' deposit accounts.[1] However, when it became public knowledge that the bank had gone to the LOLR for financing, there was a run on the bank and this triggered its collapse.

Alan Greenspan's chairmanship of the U.S. Federal Reserve left a legacy of this moral hazard principle, which was emphasized by a number of comments from the chairman himself. On several occasions he gave the market the impression that the Federal Reserve would put a floor under financial markets in general. He first did this in 1998 when dealing with the collapse of Long Term Capital Management and the fallout of the Asian crisis. Later on he would provide proactive liquidity infusions to the markets as there was a fear that Y2K would bring the financial system to a complete standstill. His views on this issue became known as the "Greenspan Put."

Next to his monetary action was his rhetoric on how a central bank should deal with bubbles. When addressing the issue during a dinner at the Economic Club of New York in December 2002, he argued, "Asset bubbles cannot be detected and monetary policy ought not to be in any case used to offset them. The collapse of bubbles can be detected, however, and monetary policy ought to be used to offset the fallout." A copy of his speech is available on the Federal Reserve's web site.

Comments and actions like this certainly encouraged subconscious thinking among banks' senior management that it was acceptable to take on ever greater risk, in the belief that if anything went wrong, ultimately

TABLE 3.1 Global Bailout Bill, 2009

Global Overview	
Country	$ Billions
United States*	14,499.0
European Union**	1,972.8
Japan	375.0
United Kingdom***	2,888.2
IMF	140.2
Total	19,875.2

*Excluding Fannie Mae and Freddie Mac.
**EURUSD 1.4.
***GBPUSD 1.60.
Source: U.S. Treasury, Federal Reserve, FDIC, IMF.

the government was there to bail them out. We emphasize that this was at most a subconscious thought.

However, this thinking came under severe criticism in the wake of the financial crash and the taxpayer-funded bailout of firms such as Citigroup, AIG, Royal Bank of Scotland, and UBS, because it gives the impression that profits within the banking industry are privatized but losses are socialized. Protecting the public's deposit monies is a noble ideal; however, bailing out banks comes with a huge cost which the taxpayer has to pay for. And the price of the 2008 bank bailout was indeed large. As of the end of 2009, the total global bill for both bailing out the banking sector and implementing the various stimulus packages had risen just below $20 trillion, of which the majority was accounted for in the United States. We summarize the figures in Table 3.1. The number for the United States excludes $5.3 trillion in guarantees that the U.S. government had to put in place to take over the liabilities of the mortgage agencies Fannie Mae and Freddie Mac.

These are numbers that are unprecedented even when compared to the inflation-adjusted levels observed during the 1930s.

Table 3.2 provides a nonexhaustive overview of the bank bailouts that were carried out during 2008–2009. We do not take into account the coordinated measures taken by central banks, such as the establishment of U.S. dollar swap lines, to ease short-term pressures in the money market in order for banks to obtain funding that had dried up in the interbank market.

TABLE 3.2   Overview of Bank Bailouts

Date	
3/16/2008	Bear Stearns is bailed out in a joint effort by J.P. Morgan and the Federal Reserve, which provides a credit line of US$30 billion.
9/7/2008	Fannie Mae and Freddie Mac are bailed out by the U.S. government with US$200 billion in preferred stock and credit lines.
9/15/2008	Lehman Brothers: too big to be rescued.
9/16/2008	AIG receives a rescue package of US$85 billion from the U.S. government.
9/25/2008	Washington Mutual comes under the control of the U.S. government; the majority of its assets are sold to J.P. Morgan.
9/29/2008	Glitnir Bank is nationalized by the Icelandic government. Mortgage lender Bradford & Bingley is nationalized by the UK government.
9/30/2008	Dexia Bank is implicitly bailed out by the Belgian government via a capital injection. The Irish government guarantees all deposits, senior and subordinated debt of all six Irish banks.
10/3/2008	Fortis Bank is split into in three parts by the Benelux governments. U.S. Congress approves Troubled Asset Relief Program (TARP) plan for US$750 billion to buy toxic assets from banks.
10/6/2008	Hypo Real Estate receives a government-facilitated credit line from the German government.
10/13/2008	Royal Bank of Scotland (RBS), HBOS, and Lloyd's receive US$64 billion from UK government. RBS and Lloyd's (which takes over HBOS) are effectively nationalized by the UK government, which now owns 70 percent and 43 percent of them, respectively. European Union commits EUR 1.3 trillion to support banks.
10/16/2008	Hungary receives a EUR 5 billion credit line from the European Central Bank (ECB).
10/28/2008	International Monetary Fund (IMF) offers a US$25 billion support package to Hungary.
1/16/2009	Bank of America receives support package from U.S. government under the form of preferred equity injection.
1/19/2009	UK government raises its stake in RBS.
2/10/2009	U.S. government announces the Public-Private Investment Program of up to US$1 trillion to purchase troubled assets.

Source: BIS 2009, www.bis.org, www.creditwritedowns.com.

Table 3.2 gives an idea of the extent of the moral hazard. The table would have been longer still if it had summarized the rescue packages that were given to the manufacturing industry in countries such as the United States and France.

In the example of the insurance industry there was clearly an objective to commit fraud. However, this was not the case in the banking industry. With most of the failures it was more of an unconscious reflex to take on greater risk with a government safety net at the back of the bankers' minds. Due to market competition, this becomes a self-fulfilling prophecy as banks compete for deposits.

However, there are cases where this safety net is exploited consciously. This was the case when Goldman Sachs and Morgan Stanley converted into commercial banks in September 2008. They were forced to make that decision due to the interbank implosion created by the Lehman Brothers collapse. It was an acknowledgment that their investment banking model had become unsustainable, and that they needed the cushion of bank deposits and the central bank LOLR. Following this move, Goldman Sachs could apply for the $700 billion government assistance money that was made available to support banks (this was the Troubled Asset Relief Program, or TARP). Goldman received a rescue package of $10 billion from the U.S. government, and with this explicit guarantee in place it proceeded to take on more risk, at precisely the moment (in the first quarter of 2009) when financial markets were at their lowest ebb and confidence.

During Q1 and Q2 of 2009 Goldman Sachs raised its value-at-risk (VaR) exposure limits to record highs, in areas such as fixed income and equity trading. This increase is shown in Table 3.3. VaR gives an indication

TABLE 3.3   Goldman Sachs VaR Limits (USD million)

Quarter End	Value at Risk (daily average)
February 2007	$ 127
May 2007	$ 133
August 2007	$ 139
November 2007	$ 151
February 2008	$ 157
May 2008	$ 184
August 2008	$ 181
November 2008	$ 197
March 2009	$ 240
June 2009	$ 245

Data source: Bloomberg.

TABLE 3.4   Goldman Sachs Net Revenue Q2 2009

Division	Net Revenue	Change (YOY)
Equity underwriting	$ 736 million	19%
Debt underwriting	336 million	25%
Fixed income, currency, and commodities	6.8 billion	186%
Investment banking advisory, mergers and acquisitions	368 million	−54%
Total trading and principle investments	$ 10.8 billion	93%

Data source: Bloomberg.

of the expected maximum loss, within a stated confidence level, that a portfolio can suffer, in this case during one trading day. As the bank increased its risk, so it increased its profits.

Nevertheless, if one takes a closer look at the drawdown of its results, it is noteworthy that the revenues are virtually completely investment banking and trading related (see Table 3.4). This was despite the fact that the firm filed for a bank license in September 2008 but does little commercial banking. The question remains whether it was justified to offer Goldman Sachs this LOLR backing. Once the firm was defined as a regular commercial bank, it had access to low-cost funding lines from the Federal Reserve, which certainly assisted the bank's trading profit.

This is an extreme example (Goldman Sachs is not one's average bank) but it highlights the moral hazard principle. Governments around the world are keen to implement stricter bank regulation, but certain players will always continue to behave as if nothing happened and continue business as usual, safe in the knowledge that they will be bailed out. If this is the case, then authorities are putting in place the wrong rules.

ADDRESSING TOO-BIG-TO-FAIL: MITIGATING MORAL HAZARD RISK

Thus, moral hazard has seemingly become an inescapable fact of life. The ultimate solution to the problem may be no more ambitious than reducing (rather than attempting to eliminate) moral hazard, without curtailing risk taking. To that end, we require new regulations. Three major issues around moral hazard and the TBTF issue need to be addressed:

1. Transparent communication by central banks about moral hazard.
2. The interconnection of financial markets and the systemic risk related to it.
3. Consolidation trends and the risks of too-big-to-fail.

We discuss each of these points individually.

Transparent Communication by Central Banks about Moral Hazard

As we noted earlier, the crisis was underpinned by a false perception that unsecured institutions, for example those that do not fall under U.S. FDIC protection, would nevertheless be regarded as TBTF by the U.S. government. This perception was first created by frequent interventions by central banks during the past four decades, and exacerbated by the rhetoric of Fed Chairman Alan Greenspan. Current Fed Chairman Ben Bernanke recognizes this issue, however, stating that "market discipline may erode further if market participants believe that, to avoid the risk of a financial crisis, the government will step in to prevent the failure of any very large institution—the 'too-big-to-fail' problem" (Bernanke 2007).

As a first step, the Federal Reserve and other central banks need to modify their rhetoric and start informing the market that there is no absolute floor under the markets, and that their expectations of being rescued must be diminished. If not, market discipline, as we have seen from Goldman Sachs, will not change. Of course this is not a short-term solution, but something that can only take place over time. Perceptions built up over 20 years do not evaporate overnight. It is important, however, that governments act now, rather than wait until the next crisis. The opportunity should be taken on a regular basis when communicating monetary policy—for example, during the press conference after Bank of England, ECB, or Federal Open Market Committee meetings, and at the Humphrey Hawkins testimonies.

In addition to the frequency of communication, its quality needs to be raised as well. General comments along the lines of "banks are at risk of losses due to excessive risk taking" are not going to change market mentality. Central banks and other institutions such as the FDIC must disclose more information on the research they are conducting on how to maintain financial stability. For example, the FDIC is doing research on procedures and methodologies in identifying which depositors it must protect and which it can impose losses on. This type of research needs a wide readership.

The most important aspect of increased communication toward the market should be in explaining how central banks undertake market stabilization efforts, and estimating future losses that have to be taken by creditors.

The Interconnection of Financial Markets and Systemic Risk

We accept that more transparent communication on its own will not solve the problem. Stronger measures are needed to reduce the frequency with which central banks and governments bail out banks.

The reason an LOLR facility is put in place is to avoid spillover effects toward other banks and ultimately prevent a bank run. Banking is ultimately a business based on confidence. The instant that customers start withdrawing their deposits on a large scale, banks are in trouble and will need to be bailed out (either by takeover or merger with another bank, or by outright support from the LOLR). The basic bank business model relies on leverage, with only a small fraction of a bank's liabilities held in reserve at the central bank. As bank funding is based on borrowing in the interbank market, systemic risk is inherent in the model.

Therefore, the authorities must place more focus on the following:

- Setting strict liquidity ratio limits, imposed by the regulator, as well as requirements to diversify funding sources, reduce reliance on single funding sources, and increase the average tenor of liabilities; the United Kingdom's Financial Services Authority (FSA) has already started the process to implement a much stricter liquidity regime for banks (FSA 2008).
- The establishment of a global central clearing agency for over-the-counter (OTC) derivatives; efforts are already underway to set this up for credit derivatives, and such a system would help to reduce bilateral counterparty risk. An alternative is for regional clearing centers based on currency.
- The establishment of a clearinghouse for the money markets, a so-called "International Money Exchange" for the interbank market that would work similarly to an exchange clearinghouse, as noted in Choudhry (2009); such a facility would serve to make the interbank market more robust during times of crisis or illiquidity, because it is at these times that banks withdraw credit lines with other banks. A central clearing mechanism that eliminated bilateral counterparty risk would make it less likely that banks would withdraw these lines.

- Reducing leverage, if necessary by regulatory fiat, through the imposition of leverage limits on banks.
- Imposing higher capital ratios than currently in place under Basel II, tailored according to the bank's size, its extent of risk exposure, and the amount of systemic risk it represents.
- Developing new capital instruments that absorb losses in distressed situations. Our recommendation is that banks promote a product that has similar features to a classic reverse convertible bond. Banks would issue so-called reverse convertible debentures, which would automatically convert into equity once the minimum capital ratio level of a bank is breached.

These measures, once implemented, would reduce the likelihood that a central bank or government would have to bail out the banks during the next economic downturn.

Consolidation Trends and the Risks of Too-Big-to-Fail

The current debate on TBTF raises the issue that such banks should be made smaller. This does appear at first glance to be a reasonable idea.

The case for this is strong when considering the Icelandic banks, which could not be rescued by their government since they had outgrown their own country's GDP. Over this past decade these banks grew from being domestic lenders to major international players. During the expansion they acquired foreign assets of almost 10 times the country's GDP (this from almost two times GDP in 2003). Furthermore, almost 80 percent of these assets were in foreign currency, making them extremely vulnerable to foreign exchange volatility. When the bubble burst, the government had to ask the IMF for an emergency loan or risk the total collapse of the banking system and thereby the economy.

However, these banks were not a major threat to the international banking system. European banks did make write-downs on the collapse of Kaupthing, Glitnir, and Landsbanki; nevertheless, the impact was not on the scale of the Lehman collapse.

The case of Ireland, which is a member of the eurozone, provides stronger backing for advocates of making banks smaller. Unlike the Icelandic banks, who decided to become international players, the Irish banks focused mainly on their home market and the United Kingdom. The Irish banking industry grew hand in hand with the domestic real estate boom. Between 1998 and 2007, house prices in real terms quadrupled on a national level. When the housing bubble burst, Irish banks were heavily exposed and, as Table 3.5 shows, their capital ratios were not robust enough to survive the

TABLE 3.5   Bank Overview of Leverage and Total Assets

Bank	2000	2001	2002	2003
JPMorgan Chase & Co.				
Total Assets	715,345	693,575	758,800	770,912
Financial Leverage	18.62	17.41	17.85	17.7
Bank of America Corp.				
Total Assets	642,191	621,764	660,951	719,483
Financial Leverage	13.87	13.16	12.99	14.06
Citigroup				
Total Assets	902,210	1,051,450	1,097,190	1,264,032
Financial Leverage	14.05	13.55	13.02	12.96
Royal Bank of Scotland				
Total Assets	320,004	368,859	412,000	454,428
Financial Leverage	18.64	16.65	17.04	18.55
HSBC Holdings				
Total Assets	674,129.90	696,079.60	758,605	1,034,216
Financial Leverage	15.69	14.9	14.82	14.2
Wells Fargo & Co.				
Total Assets	272,426	307,569	349,197	387,798
Financial Leverage	10.31	10.87	11.44	11.38
Mitsubishi UFJ Financial Group				
Total Assets	N/A	N/A	99,489.26	99,175.32
Financial Leverage	N/A	N/A	N/A	N/A
Credit Agricole Group				
Total Assets	488,221	495,067	505,718	785,731
Financial Leverage	36.37	33.35	32.89	33.33
Santander Central Hispano				
Total Assets	348,871.90	358,116.20	324,193.30	351,780.40
Financial Leverage	19.43	16.51	14.86	13.8
Goldman Sachs				
Total Assets	289,760	312,218	355,574	403,799
Financial Leverage	20.25	17.32	17.94	18.69
Lehman Brothers				
Totals Assets	224,720.00	247,816.00	260,336.00	312,061.00
Financial Leverage	32.89	31.84	31.76	28.1
Merrill Lynch				
Totals Assets	407,200.00	419,419.00	447,928.00	496,143.00
Financial Leverage	23.54	22.07	20.63	18.54
BNP Paribas				
Total Assets	693,315	825,288	710,305	782,996
Financial Leverage	33.62	32.86	30.09	27.31

2004	2005	2006	2007	2008
1,157,248	1,198,942	1,351,520	1,562,147	2,175,052
12.82	11.09	11.44	12.19	14.48
1,110,432	1,291,803	1,459,737	1,715,746	1,817,943
12.37	11.94	11.77	11.55	12.54
1,484,101	1,494,037	1,884,318	2,187,480	1,938,470
13.4	13.56	14.68	17.53	22.37
588,122	776,827	871,432	1,840,829	2,401,652
18.26	19.68	21.78	29.08	37.91
1,279,974	1,501,970	1,860,758	2,354,266	2,527,465
14.46	15.63	16.75	17.82	22.01
427,849	481,741	481,996	575,442	1,309,639
11.27	11.63	11.23	11.41	16.4
106,615.50	110,285.50	187,046.80	187,281	192,993.20
31.07	25.74	26.62	25.05	24.18
817,402	1,061,443	1,261,296	1,414,223	1,653,220
32.36	33.02	35.32	35.31	37.22
664,486.30	809,106.90	833,872.70	912,915	1,049,632
17.09	19.86	19.41	17.46	17.4
531,379	706,804	838,201	1,119,796	884,547
20.02	24.12	26.21	27.05	22.88
357,168.00	410,063.00	503,545.00	691,063.00	N/A
26.04	26.21	27.03	30.25	N/A
628,098.00	681,015.00	841,299.00	1,020,050.00	667,543.00
18.99	20.56	22.12	29.34	43.33
1,002,503	1,258,079	1,440,343	1,694,454	2,075,551
29.49	30.95	31.46	34.03	42

(Continued)

TABLE 3.5 *(Continued)*

Bank	2000	2001	2002	2003
Barclays Bank				
Total Assets	316,190	356,612	403,062	443,262
Financial Leverage	26.35	24.31	25.59	26.8
Mizuho Financial Group				
Total Assets	N/A	N/A	N/A	134,007.20
Financial Leverage	N/A	N/A	N/A	N/A
Morgan Stanley				
Total Assets	426,794	482,628	529,499	602,843
Financial Leverage	22.6	23.26	23.95	24.22
Unicredit				
Total Assets	202,655.50	208,388.10	213,349.30	238,255.60
Financial Leverage	23.45	22.77	19.53	18.06
Sumitomo Mitsui Financial Group				
Total Assets	N/A	N/A	N/A	104,586.80
Financial Leverage	N/A	N/A	N/A	N/A
ING Bank				
Total Assets	650,172	705,119	716,370	778,771
Financial Leverage	19.1	28.97	35.74	37.77
Deutsche Bank				
Total Assets	928,994	918,222	758,355	803,614
Financial Leverage	26.29	22.02	23.89	26.84
Société Générale				
Total Assets	455,881	512,499	501,265	539,224
Financial Leverage	33.7	32.9	32.2	32.07
Credit Suisse Group				
Total Assets	979,121	1,016,078	1,027,158	1,004,308
Financial Leverage	31.01	33.66	32.8	29.8
UBS				
Total Assets	1,087,552	1,253,297	1,181,118	1,386,000
Financial Leverage	27.49	26.49	29.5	34.49
Commerzbank				
Total Assets	454,904	501,312	422,134	381,585
Financial Leverage	34.85	39.38	44.9	44.9
Fortis Bank				
Total Assets	438,082.70	482,875.10	485,668	523,364.20
Financial Leverage	29.41	31.82	39.49	44.68
HBOS				
Total Assets	N/A	312,071	355,030	408,413
Financial Leverage	N/A	N/A	27.42	26.99

2004	2005	2006	2007	2008
538,181	924,357	996,787	1,227,361	2,052,980
30.44	43.93	51.61	51.62	54.76
137,750.10	143,076.20	149,612.80	149,880	154,412.10
503.63	129.51	62.49	36.81	38.85
747,334	898,523	1,121,192	1,045,409	658,812
25.44	28.68	31.83	33.63	27.56
265,406.20	787,000.30	823,284.20	1,021,835	1,045,612
18.81	21.44	21.86	19.19	18.35
102,215.20	99,731.86	107,010.60	100,858.30	111,955.90
108.7	89.01	51.84	31.7	31.38
876,391	1,158,639	1,226,307	1,312,510	1,331,663
36.46	33.47	31.8	33.64	40.97
840,068	992,161	1,584,493	2,020,349	2,202,423
30.38	32.81	41.1	51.64	62.33
601,355	835,134	956,841	1,071,762	1,130,003
32.46	34.64	34.4	36.04	34.77
1,089,485	1,339,052	1,255,956	1,360,680	1,170,350
29.8	30.98	30.28	30.15	33.52
1,737,118	2,058,348	2,396,511	2,274,891	2,014,815
45.01	48.69	47.54	53.97	61.81
424,877	444,861	608,278	616,474	625,196
42.79	38.73	39.09	41.7	36.11
614,085.30	728,994.50	775,229	871,179	92,870
41.9	39.2	38.01	30.66	24.2
448,165	540,873	591,813	666,947	689,917
26.91	28.92	29.94	29.87	40.08

(Continued)

TABLE 3.5   *(Continued)*

Bank	2000	2001	2002	2003
Dexia				
Total Assets	257,726	351,250	350,692	349,463
Financial Leverage	42.6	41.28	40.82	38.42
Lloyds TSB Group				
Total Assets	219,113	235,793	252,561	252,012
Financial Leverage	21.24	22.32	26.69	28.72
KBC Group				
Total Assets	187,658	227,759.20	221,730.50	225,586.80
Financial Leverage	34.42	31.21	28.16	25.45

Data source: Bloomberg.

shock. The Irish government was forced to provide explicit backing for its banks; one impact of this was that the Ireland sovereign rating was cut from AAA, on fears that the public sector debt liability created by the guarantees would become unsustainable. Ultimately the majority of Irish banks were effectively nationalized. The Irish situation was not that dramatic compared to the Icelandic one for a simple reason: Ireland had the safety net of the eurozone. This in itself exposed eurozone taxpayers to potential losses if the government itself had needed to be bailed out.

Despite the deleveraging process that has been taking place since the start of the crisis, some major international banks are still bigger than their own country's GDP. This is certainly the case for the Swiss banks UBS and Credit Suisse. At the end of 2008 Credit Suisse's balance sheet was 2.72 times and UBS's 4.18 times the GDP of Switzerland (see Tables 3.5 and 3.6).

Table 3.5 also proves that (contrary to popular belief) European banks were and still are more leveraged than U.S. banks, and that no UK or German bank outgrew its country's GDP.

However, in countries such as the Netherlands and Belgium one can notice a similar pattern to that in Switzerland. The Dutch bank ING clearly became TBTF for the government as its total assets were 1.53 times the GDP of the Netherlands. This was also the reason why, in the case of Fortis Bank, the Benelux countries implemented a joint rescue plan to save it.

While in principle we agree with the idea of breaking up banks that are too large, there are practical difficulties with so doing. First, what metric would be used to determine whether a bank is too big? A simplistic measure of looking at the total size of assets on the balance sheet is not the answer.

It is perfectly plausible that a bank's total assets increase via organic growth. In this case it would be unfair to penalize this development,

2004	2005	2006	2007	2008
388,787	508,761	566,743	604,564	651,006
33.46	32.98	37.15	40.29	67.66
284,422	309,754	343,598	353,346	436,033
25.95	27.97	30.6	29.92	36.66
285,163	325,801	325,400	355,597	355,317
23.78	21.76	19.86	19.81	22.53

TABLE 3.6   GDP per Country

Country	GDP $ Millions
United States	14,264,600
Japan	4,923,761
Germany	3,667,513
France	2,865,737
United Kingdom	2,674,085
Italy	2,313,893
Spain	1,611,767
Netherlands	868,940
Belgium	506,392
Switzerland	492,595
Ireland	273,248

Source: IMF.

certainly where the quality of assets are perfectly matched with outstanding liabilities. To make a comparison, one would not necessarily break up the U.S. retail distributor Wal-Mart or the UK supermarket chain Tesco simply because either had a dominant market position. That said, neither of these corporate institutions is relying on the LOLR, and neither represents any kind of systemic risk to the economy.

But where regulators have a stronger case is in the area of growth through merger and/or acquisition. When this takes place, regulators must look closely at how the transaction is funded. It is now obvious that Royal Bank of Scotland and Fortis suffered as a result of taking over ABN Amro without having a waterproof funding strategy in place behind the transaction.

Even a smaller size of bank is no guarantee that systemic risk would diminish. Some banks are small in assets but still impose a huge risk for a potential run on the banking system. Northern Rock and Bear Stearns were very good examples of that. So it becomes important that a range of quantitative and qualitative assessments be made before one can decide that a bank has become too big. Central banks, which have a considerable amount of private information at hand, are in a position to make that judgment call. However, a policy maker who needs to streamline this decision into a simple metric legal framework is less capable of doing this.

There is also the issue of what to do with banks that are already too big. This would mean that they have to be broken up. The question then is who will buy the assets? At what price are they going to be sold? These are not insurmountable problems; they simply need careful consideration. We recommend that as far as possible, viable business lines are hived off into stand-alone operations under existing management. This would be perfectly feasible in the case of most multinational banking groups, which often take over overseas banking chains as a complete whole.

When governments succeed in breaking up big banks, they will face substantial pressure not to allow these companies to grow too large again. There is precedent for this in other industries; for example, the breakup of AT&T in the United States. This triggered subsequent mergers among other telecommunication firms, which then became large organizations. In the United States there is legislation in place to block a bank merger or acquisition if the bank is left with more than 10 percent of the total deposit base of the market. We recommend a similar cap in other countries.

It is evident that certain banks became too big during the past 10 years, to the extent that the prosperity of a country and its citizens was placed in jeopardy. The best examples were Citigroup and RBOS. There was a side negative impact as well, as big banks lost focus on the relationship side. The banking sector is in theory still synonymous with being a financial *service* industry; however, it appears that over the years the people in the business neglected service in their business model. Putting the clients' needs first should become a priority again, and to do this we will need a change in approach and emphasis among bank senior management.

Keeping the size of banks in check should first be achieved by keeping quantitative measures, such as liquidity and leverage ratios, under strict limits as previously suggested. However, if regulators do not succeed in keeping banks in line using these restrictions, then downsizing the total asset size of a bank below a certain percentage of the GDP of its own country must become the solution of last resort.

MACROPRUDENTIAL REGULATION: REGULATING BANK SYSTEMIC RISK

The art of banking remains unchanged from when banks were first established. At its core are the two principles of asset-liability mismatch and liquidity risk management. The act of undertaking loans and deposits creates the mismatch, because while investors like to lend for as short a term as possible, borrowers prefer to borrow for as long a term as possible. This also gives rise to liquidity risk, and bankers are therefore required to take steps to ensure that liquidity, the ability to roll over funding of long-dated loans, is continuously available.

The fact that all banks, irrespective of their size, approach, or strategy, must manage these two basic principles means that they are, ultimately, identical institutions. They deal within the same markets and with each other. That means that the bankruptcy of any one bank, while serious for its customers and creditors, can have a bigger impact still on the wider economy because of the risk this poses to other banks. It is this systemic risk that posed the danger for the world's economies in 2008, after Lehman Brothers collapsed, and which remains a challenge for financial regulators.

In this section we consider the role of government in the financial system in the post–credit crunch era. We also examine the nature of bank systemic risk, and present suggestions on how to manage it most effectively.

Systemic Risk: Defining Systemic Importance

The economic importance of banks is evident from the reaction of Western governments to the crisis following the collapse of U.S. firms AIG and Lehman Brothers. Banks such as Citibank, Royal Bank of Scotland, UBS, and KBC Bank were partly nationalized and/or received large cash injections from their governments. These were the institutions deemed too big to fail (TBTF), and whose bankruptcy, it was viewed, would have been catastrophic for the world economy because of the high systemic risk such bankruptcy represented.

This raises the question as to exactly which banks are systemically risky. The events of 2007–2009 suggest that not only large banks present systemic risk. Prior to September 2008, the experience of Bear Stearns in the United States and Northern Rock in the United Kingdom had shown that banks not necessarily defined as TBTF could nevertheless create significant market turbulence when they failed. This implies that in a globalized economy with many interconnections, the collapse of almost any bank, and certainly any bank with cross-border interests, can destabilize the economy. Banks therefore must not only manage their own risks adequately, but they also have to be aware of the potential risk exposure of their counterparties. Bear Stearns, for example, had large exposure to hedge funds that had invested in low-grade assets.

The UK Financial Services Authority (FSA) has suggested that a firm be defined as systemically important as follows:

> . . . *when its collapse would impair the provision of credit and financial services to the market with significant negative consequences for the real economy.*[2]

Thus, the precise definition of systemic importance is no longer purely a reflection of the size of the bank. The FSA view of the factors that make firms systemically important includes the following:

- Systemic by size: The absolute size of the bank is relevant, but so is its size relative to a particular financial market or product.
- Systemic by interconnection: the importance of the firm to the interbank market and clearing systems.
- Systemic by association: where the market views one company as representative of a group, whereupon failure by one is seen as a potential failure by all (an example would be the UK building society sector).

The FSA view is a logical approach. However, it remains the judgment of financial regulators to determine the extent to which a particular firm falls into one or more of the three categories and can be specified as systemically important. For maximum risk mitigation it is necessary to minimize the amount of judgment required. In this regard, therefore, there is a strong case for suggesting that almost all banks fall into at least the last category (systemic by association), making virtually all banks potential areas of material systemic risk. If we accept this, then there are significant implications for bank supervisory authorities.

Macroprudential Regulation

The events of 2007–2009 demonstrated clearly how the failure of one bank can have significant implications for other banks as well as for the entire market. As a generalization, banks are identical entities. Large numbers of them operate in the same markets, with the same customers, and with each other. It is this interconnection that means that when one bank fails, the entire industry (and by extension the economy) is at risk. Hence, it is not sufficient for financial regulators to aim to ensure that each bank is properly managed and has sufficient capital and liquidity arrangements in place. They also have to oversee the soundness of the industry as a whole. Thus, *macroprudential* regulation is now the main focus for bank regulators.

The framework within which macroprudential regulation would be undertaken remains under discussion (for example, see Bank of England [2009]). The broad objective of such regulation is to ensure the continued safe running of the financial system in the event of individual bank failure. A number of steps can be taken by regulators to assist with this.

In the first instance, bank business activity would benefit from being controlled by regulators to the extent that it becomes less cyclical, or less susceptible to the ill disciplines of a bull market. When the economy is growing steadily and risk aversion is decreasing, banks fall into a pattern of lowering loan origination standards and easing the supply of credit. A booming economy and tightening credit spreads alter bank risk-taking behavior. The typical reaction is a lowering of loan origination standards and a change in banks' strategy to the extent that market share and higher return-on-equity (ROE) targets become emphasized, sometimes to the detriment of liquidity and capital management. This was the error made by UK banks such as Northern Rock, Bradford & Bingley, and HBOS.[3]

The supply of plentiful and cheap credit helps boost the price of assets such as equities and real estate. At the end of the cycle and in a recession, banks then as a group withdraw credit on a large scale, widening the impact of the recession and also causing a fall in asset prices. Because banks operate in the same markets and with each other, this cyclical pattern is exacerbated during any significant market event.

The first requirement in macroprudential regulation, therefore, is for banks to operate in a less cyclical manner. This can be enforced by altering bank capital and liquidity requirements. At any time when the market is viewed as pursuing ever more risky asset generation, and/or credit is seen as too easily available, the regulator can require banks to:

- Increase their level of capital, particularly Tier 1 equity capital.
- Adjust their liquidity ratio to ensure that there is less reliance on short-term funding and wholesale interbank funding.[4]

Both of these steps would increase the cost of doing business for a bank, and thereby lead to decreased lending levels during a boom period.

The difficulty, of course, is the judgment call of when exactly a bull market is under way, or the precise moment when a market is, to borrow an earlier phrase, irrationally exuberant. While it is easy to see in hindsight at what point a market crash began, it is harder to call such an event beforehand. Measures that regulators may wish to consider include:

- The overall level of lending in the economy, both as an absolute level and as a percentage of GDP.
- The rate of increase in retail lending, for example credit card and residential mortgage approvals, as well as the rate of increase in lower-credit-quality lending.
- The rates of return on equity on bank capital, and whether this is running at above long-run averages.

In practice, the regulator may wish to use a combination of these measures when making this assessment, which will always remain a judgment call. It would also need to monitor aggregate economic indicators such as the rate of growth of GDP and asset prices, compared to medium-term average rates.

The Bank of England has suggested that particular types of loan activity need to be targeted when capital requirements are raised.[5] Otherwise, there is the risk that banks will merely pull back from lower-risk business lines and use the capital savings created to continue business in higher-risk activity. This is logical, and we would suggest that it may be addressed by focusing—not at the macroprudential level but at the direct individual bank level—on ROE targets and leverage levels. If regulators place limits on these two values, and alter them to suit the business cycle, this will also drive more countercyclical behavior. What is apparent is that a reliance on higher capital requirements alone may not be a sufficient safeguard against systemic risk, because it would be difficult to ascertain what level of capital was enough.[6] The liquidity ratio for a bank is a key risk measure and regulators can use it to influence macroprudential behavior. By setting a more conservative liquidity ratio requirement for banks that run large asset-liability gaps, and therefore greater liquidity risk, the regulator can ensure that asset origination cannot exceed by too much the ability of the bank to fund such assets more robustly.

Notwithstanding the view that essentially all banks pose a systemic risk of a kind, due to their interconnectivity, as the cases of Citigroup and RBS showed, the risk from larger multinational banks may be mitigated by specific stringent treatment. The FSA has suggested that each legal entity in a banking group could be required to set up a "living will" so that it could be easily and safely unwound without affecting the capital base of the rest of the group. This is not a risk mitigator, however, but merely a means by which the impact of failure can be concentrated into a shorter timescale. To effectively control the risk of TBTF banks, one approach could be to require them to ensure that their overseas operations are separately capitalized and liquidity self-sufficient. This would reduce the risk that an economic crisis in one country could be imported into another via the banking system.

In this last regard, the requirement to have separately capitalized trading and retail divisions would be beneficial. A large group entity that relies on the central bank LOLR is a direct risk to the taxpayer, and its failure has significant impact, as we noted with the examples of Citibank, RBS, KBC Bank, and UBS in the United States, United Kingdom, Belgium, and Switzerland, respectively, during 2008. Table 3.5 shows the growth in size, leverage, and potential risk of these banks in the buildup to the Lehman bankruptcy, following which they all had to be bailed out by their governments. We can observe the steadily increasing risk exposure, particularly with regard to leverage ratios.

If a banking group's risk-taking arm gets into difficulties, in theory if it is a separately capitalized entity it can be unwound or allowed to fail without endangering the retail banking arm. Its subsidiarity would also enforce funding discipline as lenders would lend to it at a premium over the parent entity funding rate. There is, therefore, a strong case for requiring the trading arm to be a separate subsidiary with its own capital base.

Recommended Policy Approach

Effective macroprudential regulation requires that banks also take specific measures as part of the effort to maintain systemic stability. We suggest that best-practice thinking is for measures along the following lines:

- Reducing market exposure to large systemically important banks by requiring them to make a larger proportion of their trades via a centralized clearing system. This would reduce contagion across the market when one bank failed, as a central clearinghouse reduces bilateral counterparty risk.
- Requiring the trading arms of all banks to hold more capital than the retail arms. This is expected in a new Basel III regulatory capital regime. Trading arms should also be separately capitalized legal entities.
- Requiring a higher capital ratio for large banks, and enforcing a leverage ratio.
- Establishing cross-border stability arrangements. Given that uniform arrangements worldwide are unlikely to be implemented, enforce regulation that the home country of a banking group structured across subsidiaries in different national jurisdictions should not be responsible

for saving the whole group. The practical impact of this is that subsidiaries must be stand-alone entities, both capital and liquidity self-sufficient, which could be allowed to fail without endangering the entire group.

More stringent macroprudential and micro-level regulation would provide for greater financial market stability at the time of the next recession, more so because the nature and size of the next crisis cannot be estimated with any certainty. At the micro level, systemic risk will be mitigated by requiring all banks to adhere to a more stringent capital and liquidity regime, and one that has a countercyclical emphasis. Both of these requirements will increase the cost of doing business, and thus reduce lending volumes in the long run, but regulatory authorities and governments will view this as a desirable result because it will reduce the ability for a bank to grow rapidly during a bull market as well as reduce the need for it to cut lending during a recession. As the natural inclination for a private company is to maximize return and minimize operating costs, countercyclical behavior would not occur in a completely free market. To enforce it will therefore require regulatory fiat.

CONCLUSION

The 2007–2009 financial crash and recession, and its aftermath, demonstrated that governments deem the banking system to play an important role in the development of the world's economy. This places the industry outside the realm of a purely private free enterprise, because of the significant impact of individual failure on the wider economy. The current state of affairs combines government guarantees of the Western banking system with potentially significant moral hazard. This arrangement became necessary to prevent collapse in the global economy following the Lehman default, when it appeared that many Western banks were about to fail. In the foreseeable future we do not expect that the current market structure will change.

The current system essentially allows banks to take as much risk exposure as they wish in order to maximize profit, with the knowledge that should they incur large losses they will be bailed out. Given the risks that such moral hazard implies, it becomes important for governments and regulators to act decisively to mitigate these risks. The conclusion from this is that regulators need to review the adequacy of macroprudential regulation, enforced by the central authorities, to ensure the stability of the banking sector throughout the business cycle.

We have proposed three areas in which policy makers should implement strict rules as part of a new bank business model, which will reduce the likelihood that the LOLR has to intervene during the next economic downturn. The key to efficient macroprudential regulatory oversight is to require banks to follow countercyclical behavior with regard to capital, liquidity, and loan origination. In addition, infrastructure must be enhanced to reduce the level of interconnectivity in the system, via centralized clearinghouses. This would help to reduce counterparty risk and lower the impact of bank failures.

CHAPTER 4

Corporate Governance and Remuneration in the Banking Industry

Corporate governance in the banking industry was severely criticized in the aftermath of the financial crisis of 2007–2009. Much of the debate centered on banks' remuneration, although the failures in corporate governance were not limited to the bonus culture, which in reality had little connection with the causes of the crisis. More relevant causal factors that should be looked at included the type of representatives on the board, the expertise of these board members, and the partnerships of investment banks.

In this chapter we review the failings of bank corporate governance during the buildup to the crisis, and present recommendations for improvements to the model.

BONUSES AND A MORAL DILEMMA

The bonus culture is the first topic that is raised when talking about bank corporate governance. The bonuses that have been paid out to investment bankers are objectionable in the eyes of many legislators and the mainstream media, and came under populist attack after banks had to be rescued with taxpayer money. This became an emotional debate which has the potential to lead to flawed decision making that could jeopardize the future prospects of the banking industry. Therefore this is also the most controversial and sensitive chapter in this book.

We should be careful about automatically condemning bonuses. As Jack Welch, the former CEO of General Electric, once noted, it is important to reward the outperformers. These are people who make the difference in corporate performance. In a free-market capitalist system we need such people as these, on the one hand, but on the other hand society also needs a safety net for those who fall out of the system. However, for the continued success of the system we must be careful not to level out the high performers, who continuously lift standards and boundaries. Instead of discouraging such people, society actually needs to encourage them, as without them there would be less for governments and citizens to share.

That said, it is unarguable that there were and still are unjustifiable excesses and distortions in the remuneration system employed at banks. Of course, the problems discussed elsewhere in this book, including failures in regulation, bank liquidity management, credit standards, and excess leverage, are more to blame for causing the crisis than the bonus culture. The argument that high bonuses were the incentive to adopt extreme leverage and poor liquidity standards is a sophism. The impression that bankers would sit together in a meeting room discussing the potential bonus they could take home if they set up a structured investment vehicle (SIV) or a collateralized debt obligation squared (CDO-squared) is simply wrong. That is not how the system works. It would be more correct to argue that high remuneration arose from the mistakes that were made in the other areas, but which are not being made a scapegoat. In fact, to concentrate on bonuses is to abrogate the responsibility for the real errors that were made in banks, central banks, and government.

Notwithstanding this state of affairs, it is true that in certain cases there was greed involved and that this greed skewed decision making. But this is not limited to the banking industry. Consider, for example, the events at WorldCom, the excesses of CEO Dennis Kozlowski from Tyco, and of course the Enron saga, which led to the demise of that company's audit firm Arthur Andersen.[1]

A DISTORTED REMUNERATION MODEL

Greed is undoubtedly, since prehistory, a trait of humankind. But of course this does not mean that we should simply accept it and close our eyes to certain practices.

Let us consider first the type of malpractices that occurred in the banking industry. A major issue connected with excessive risk taking at banks is the tendency to calculate the net present value (NPV) of the future profits made on deals, and add this to the annual profit-and-loss (P&L) budget of a sales or trading desk. The following hypothetical example is typical of what occurs regularly at many investment banks.

A salesperson closes a transaction with a client that is a 20-year inflation hedge, for an amount of €250 million. The future cash flows over that period would create a profit of €4.5 million, which would be a substantial contribution to the salesperson's annual budget. However, the €4.5 million will be realized over the lifetime of the deal (that is, 20 years) and represents a net present value. There is always the possibility that during the next 20 years the client could go bankrupt and be incapable of fulfilling its liabilities. Potentially this could mean that the bank would be stuck with a negative mark-to-market on the transaction that could not be recovered from the client. If we assume this happens three years into the deal, then unwinding the transaction would create a loss of €1.3 million for the bank.

The problem, however, is that the salesperson would in all probability have already been remunerated on this deal three years earlier. And furthermore, as is not unusual in the industry, it is also possible that the salesperson has left the bank and is no longer an employee. A transaction that the salesperson originated and received additional compensation for (in addition to his annual salary) has now created a loss for the bank that paid him.

These practices have been abandoned at certain banks, which have replaced them with a system whereby part of the profit realized on long-dated transactions is placed in a reserve account and allocated to the budget of the trader or salesperson on a year-by-year basis as long as the trade remains profitable.

Nevertheless, there are still many banks that do not apply this system and stimulate instead something akin to hit-and-run behavior. The preceding example refers to a long-dated inflation swap, but similar parallels can be made with the selling or trading of collateralized debt obligations (CDOs) and other structured credit deals that have maturities of 7 to 10 years or even longer. In the case of the CDO-type product, the authors are familiar with examples where the profit or fees paid out to sales desks were dependent on the quality of the tranche of the note that was sold. At a Belgian bank, salespeople received a 5 percent commission of the notional of the tranche added to their P&L budget whenever they sold to an investor client the BB+ tranche of a CDO, which is the poorest quality (just above the equity tranche) of the structure. Investors in a BB+ note, one would hope, are always sophisticated market participants who understand fully the risk/reward behavior of such products. But this is not always the case. And such a remuneration arrangement can stimulate potentially reckless behavior. For instance, what if the desk, spurred on by such a remuneration arrangement, starts selling CDO tranches to clients of its commercial paper desk? A CDO tranche is not in the first instance a suitable investment for money-market investors.

Is this greed? To a certain extent it is. But it is the natural outcome of a system in which senior management does not look at the quality of

P&L realized by its traders or salespersons, but rather its immediate impact. What system should be adopted? Is there a benefit for the bank and all stakeholders if instead of closing, for instance, 5,000 tickets with low margins in order to realize its budget, a trading desk closes 10 to 15 deals that generate a similar profit? This type of mentality created the possibility that some fixed-income sales desks would focus only on high-commission deals and would neglect the daily plain-vanilla flow business.

Nevertheless, we must still downplay the hysteria about big bonuses. Only a very small minority of bank employees receive excessive remuneration packages. (Then again, everything is relative.) For example, during the period 2002–2007 approximately 4,000 people in the city of London received a bonus greater than £1 million.[2] Out of a total of approximately 325,000 people in London employed in financial services, this is only 1 percent of the total population. In this respect the state of affairs in the financial industry is replicated in other industries.

This does not mean that there are not certain anomalies. An interesting observation was made by Clementi, Richardson, and Walter (in Acharya and Richardson 2009), to wit that something is not quite right when board members' remuneration is higher than the return from the underlying stock or the return earned by shareholders, who ultimately take the risk. Or the way they phrased it: "Would you rather manage a Wall Street firm or own the shares in one?"

Their analysis produced some surprising results. First of all, they compared the total remuneration package of CEOs among several industries (mining, manufacturing, transport, wholesale, retail, and the financial industry, including the insurance sector). A first observation is that the average wealth of a CEO in the financial industry outperforms that of other industries.[3] This comes as no surprise as this was already a general belief. Second—and this could explain at first glance why the performances are higher compared to other sectors—CEOs in the financial industry receive a higher amount of company shares.

Given this feature, one would think their wealth would be much more related to the performance of the underlying share. However, if one looks at the relationship between the wealth of CEOs and shareholders one observes surprising results. The authors measured the extent to which CEOs' wealth would change if the shareholders' wealth would rise by 1 percent—in other words, the elasticity of CEOs' wealth versus shareholders' wealth. Apparently CEOs' wealth is less affected in this case compared to shareholders' wealth performance. And this answers the earlier question: In a downturn market, CEOs' wealth is less affected than that of shareholders. This we understand goes against the fair principles of capitalism. CEOs are guiding the firm, with the backing from the shareholders, and are taking risks to produce profit. But if their strategy does not work out, they should be penalized to the same extent as the shareholders.

UNSUITABLE PERSONAL BEHAVIOR

As in certain other industries, as well as in the world of politics, the investment banking industry attracts personalities with a more than healthy interest in acquiring wealth and control. These individuals are often more driven, and more motivated, than those around them and consequently it is not unusual to see these types promoted to senior positions.

Senior management in banking is from time to time dominated by eccentric personalities who manage strategic desks or indeed the entire firm. This is evident from Sorkin (2009) and McDonald and Robinson (2009).

Reading about the Lehman collapse, one repeatedly comes across the remark that former Lehman CEO Dick Fuld and his president, Joe Gregory, did not give the impression that they understood the risks involved in the new investment banking environment from the 1990s onward. In the two references just noted, the words *remote* and *denial* are often used when describing the personalities of the top two Lehman executives. What is implied—which, if true, would be worrying if it is repeated in other banks' management—is that these shortcomings were often due to megalomania, excessive ego, and envy.

An example of this is given in McDonald and Robinson (2009), describing the way Dick Fuld dealt with the rise of the private equity firm Blackstone, which was run by two ex-Lehman managing directors, Peter Peterson and Stephen Schwarzman, who it appears were not on speaking terms with the Lehman CEO. Instead of focusing on the core business and listening to the advice of his senior investment banking team (Larry McCarthy, Mike Gelband, and Alex Kirk), who had been warning since 2005 about the growing risks that Lehman was facing, Fuld was driven by frustration and envy to start investing in hedge funds, energy companies, credit cards, commodities, and leveraged mortgages, apparently not only to match the success of the private equity firm, but also because of a desire to top the league tables published on Wall Street. This obsession arose to such irrational levels that at certain times when strategic acquisitions were being discussed at the executive committee, the head of risk management was asked to leave the room. Clearly, if we accept this anecdote as fact, this is not only worrying but also extremely dangerous for any firm.

It is certainly possible to run a big organization without getting into detail on the technicalities of the operation. Genuinely effective business leaders are wise to surround themselves with experts and talented people who can guide them into making the right decisions and have the personality to motivate their troops. However, from the moment that ego is prioritized over all else, then an organization is in great danger. This danger is exacerbated if the person at the top is surrounded by sycophantic acolytes whose only purpose would appear to be simply to keep the monarchy in place.

It is difficult, from a corporate governance point of view, to make recommendations or formulate regulations on how to deal with these types of phenomena. At the end of the day it is not up to the government or regulator to remove such people, or better still not to promote them in the first place, but rather up to the shareholders to vote them out of the organization.

CONCLUSION

In order to tackle these excesses and incentives of unnecessary risk taking, we recommend that remuneration policy should have some long-term prospects built into it.

One such policy that is noteworthy is in place at two European banks with which the authors are familiar. The UK FSA is considering imposing a similar system at the banks it regulates. The bonus is split up into three parts. For ease of discussion let's say this split is in equal thirds. The first part of the bonus is a straightforward cash payment, paid out immediately. The second part of the remuneration package is in the form of shares of stock options that have to be held for a minimum period of time before they can be sold or exercised. That period should be around three years. The final part of the bonus, also in cash, is placed in a claw-back account, which is also monitored for three years. During that period the bank has the right to reclaim part of this cash back if a trade or deal originated by the individual concerned starts losing money for the bank.[4]

A bonus arrangement with postponement of cash payouts would certainly diminish a hit-and-run mentality among traders and sales. However, one should not forget that this system would not prevent a crash or crisis of the kind we experienced in 2007–2009. If this bonus schedule had been common practice during the beginning of the twenty-first century it would not have prevented some traders and salespersons from receiving considerable amounts of money, even when it would have been spread out over, say, 2003 to 2007. The subprime mortgage crash was created by the buildup of a number issues acting over a decade.

Another initiative that should be investigated is the return of partnerships of the kind that operated on Wall Street and in London among the

U.S. investment banks and UK merchant banks. It would be difficult to prove empirically, but if partnerships had still existed today, it is possible that senior management would have thought twice before pursuing certain risky strategies. Accounting firms still operate under this model, and a partner at an audit firm company will be careful before signing off on a balance sheet of an audited client, as the partner can be held legally responsible if the information on the balance sheet does not reflect reality. So the question that should be asked is whether it would make sense to return to this model in investment banking. We believe that risk-taking behavior of senior bankers would be more contained if they were personally liable should a transaction go wrong, as was the case in the past. However, such a model may be unworkable in today's global market and large multinational integrated banks.

Risk behavior is also closely related to the type of representatives on the board. This is not a discussion that is limited to the banking industry, but can be generalized for the corporate world. Board members represent the shareholders. Increased transparency forces listed companies to report their results on a quarterly basis. There is nothing wrong with this. Nevertheless, the very short-term focus on corporate results makes board members focus on the share price. The issue here is that on the boards of banks and companies there are rarely, if ever, members that represent the bondholders (in case the company has outstanding debt).

Having only people on the board who are mostly concerned about a rising share price will certainly influence risk behavior and culture, which always resonates downward from the feelings and beliefs of the highest level. If major investors in the outstanding debt of a company were to have a presence on the board, the accent on policies and strategies would be more risk contained.

There is also the issue of the expertise of board members. Certainly in banks the sophistication of financial products reached a high level over time. There are well-known anecdotes of board members of European bailed-out banks who were not up to speed with, for example, securitization techniques and structured credit in general. The authors are personally familiar with senior management at European banks who displayed this lack of knowledge of modern banking.

Therefore we recommend that regulators monitor the financial knowledge of all board members and force them to take relevant courses on a regular basis, in order that they stay updated about developments in the industry.

CHAPTER 5

Bank Capital Safeguards: Additional Capital Buffers and Reverse Convertibles

One of the lessons learned from the financial crash of 2007–2009 is the importance of having sufficient capital buffers built into a bank's balance sheet, in order to be sufficiently prepared for an economic downturn. In this respect additional capital reserves should be set aside in times of economic booms and prosperity, in so-called *countercyclical* capital management. We recognize that such reserves would not in any way prevent an economic slowdown or market correction; however, they would smooth out the aftermath of a crisis and do more to prevent a banking system collapse. As a consequence, actions from a lender of last resort (LOLR) would become necessary on fewer occasions, and hence the final bill for the taxpayer would be lower. Larger capital buffers and countercyclical capital provisioning should be viewed as an extra parachute available to prevent a hard landing.

This chapter discusses ways of improving bank capital management and reviews an instrument that can assist in this process: the reverse convertible bond.

CAPITAL ISSUES IN A BEAR MARKET

From the timeline in Chapter 1 we saw that many banks got into trouble when they were forced to raise additional capital once their capital ratios dropped below regulatory thresholds. However, the problem at that point was the difficulty of going to the capital markets and raising the required funds, because at that point investor risk aversion was in full play. Tier 1 and 2 regulatory capital becomes extremely expensive in such a situation, due to the higher default probability that investors perceive in times of crises.

This drop in capital is therefore also why the leverage ratio rises. In Table 3.5 (Bank Overview of Leverage and Total Assets) we showed that for some banks such as Deutsche Bank and UBS financial leverage rose considerably during 2008. This was not because these banks continued to expand their balance sheets, but simply because of the rise in losses on mortgage loans which eroded their available capital. Automatically the banks' leverage increased. A similar phenomenon was observed during the downfall of the hedge fund LTCM in 1998. At a certain moment the fund's leverage ratio was at 100 percent. This was not due to the fact that the fund kept on increasing positions, but arose because of depletion of the firm's capital against outstanding assets.

This consequence intensifies the downward spiral as banks see their net worth decline further and so tighten their loan origination standards as they withdraw from the market. Credit becomes scarcer and logically very expensive. A shift takes place between the credit supply from the bank's side and credit demand from the corporate borrower's side. This results in a slowing down in business investment and a downward spiral that pushes the economy into a deep recession. This sequence of events is known as the *financial accelerator*.[1]

Banks such as Citigroup, Wachovia, Merrill Lynch, Morgan Stanley, and RBS, to name a few, became victims of this vicious circle during 2007–2009. Bear Stearns was rescued at the last minute by a joint effort of the U.S. Federal Reserve and JPMorgan Chase in a combined LOLR effort, but this action was unfortunately not extended to Lehman Brothers, whose resulting failure triggered a severe bank crisis.

Surprisingly for some observers, during this crisis Spanish banks (as well as Canadian and Australian banks) remained relatively unaffected. The major reason for this was that the Spanish regulator had implemented a framework that forced banks to put aside additional capital reserves for some years before the bubble burst. This process is better known as *dynamic provisioning*.

The regime in Spain placed an emphasis on prudent trading and strict risk management procedures. Also, the fact that Spanish banks were required to consolidate all derivative instruments onto their balance sheet, so that vehicles such as synthetic collateralized debt obligations (CDOs) or structured investment vehicles (SIVs) could not be used to place exposure off the balance sheet, contributed to a more robust banking industry that was better protected against market downturns. The regulatory regimes in Canada and Australia, which emphasized a more conservative liquidity management regime and leverage limits, also helped prevent a banking crisis in those two countries.

LOOKING FOR NEW CAPITAL INSTRUMENTS

To deal with the tension that arises between the philosophy of dynamic provisioning and the way that accounting standards deal with provisioning, the International Accounting Standards Board (IASB) adopted the methods of the Spanish banking regulator and ruled that it would move toward a system of provisions based on expected losses. In the environment prevailing in 2008, accounting rules only allowed provisions for losses already incurred on loan portfolios. In the case of dynamic provisioning a collective assessment of impairment is needed. This means that one has to evaluate the number of damaged loans in a portfolio that has not yet been identified as being impaired.[2]

Fine-tuning or developing new capital market instruments can also help to establish extra capital buffers for banks. Gary Stern (2009)[3] and, in an earlier paper, Mark Flannery (2002) have published recommendations in this field which we consider in detail here.[4]

The recommendation for strengthening the capital buffer makes use of the basic techniques of an existing instrument, which is the reversed convertible (RC) bond. This is a hybrid instrument that has the features of a standard convertible bond, which combines a plain-vanilla corporate bond with equity. Initially the investor buys a classic corporate bond, but with a potential obligation to receive a predetermined number of shares of the issuing company at maturity in the event that the stock price of the company hits a specified (knock-in) level, which would be below the level of the stock price at the time of issue. In return for this obligation the investor receives a higher coupon compared to that payable on a vanilla bond with the same maturity and from the same issuer. This higher coupon is a reflection of the premium of the embedded put option that is built into the bond, which the investor has in effect shorted. The rule of thumb is that the higher the coupon, the higher the probability the bond will be converted into shares.[5]

The product recommended in Flannery's original paper would have similar features to the RC bond. Rather than being linked to the stock price, though, in this case the special RC (SRC) issued by a bank would have conversion triggered automatically whenever the bank's regulatory capital ratio fell below a specified level. The trigger to convert the bonds into equity would reduce the pressure of insolvency that weighs on banks during a downward cycle, as raising new capital is extremely difficult in a risk-averse environment.

The major characteristics of the SRC are as follows:

- The automatic trigger is linked to regulatory capital ratio level.
- As long as no conversion has taken place, the SRC remains a subordinated debt instrument where interest rates are tax deductible (note that

under the new Basel III rules, this would be Tier 2 capital, but on conversion the funds would become Tier 1 capital).

- The strike price would be the market share price at the moment of conversion.
- The triggering event would be based upon the market share price.
- There are no callable features for either the issuer or the investor.
- At maturity or in case of conversion into equity, the bank needs to issue immediately a new SRC to replace the old one.

If an SRC-type instrument was acceptable to the regulator (and note that there is precedent for this—in the United Kingdom the FSA has accepted as Tier 2 capital the convertible bonds issued by Lloyds TSB Bank in 2009 that have similar features to an SRC), we expect that the regulator would define a minimum and maximum percentage of this SRC instrument that could be held by banks on their balance sheets.

For illustration we consider a hypothetical numerical example where the minimum level of SRCs is 4 percent of total assets. We also assume that the minimum capital ratio is raised to 10 percent by the regulators. In this case there is a 40 percent buffer or reserve in case the 10 percent equity level is eroded.

Figure 5.1 represents the simplified balance sheet of a bank at different points in time, taking into account a hypothetical minimum regulatory capital ratio of 10 percent and the assumption that the regulator would require a 4 percent minimum of SRCs on the balance sheet. N is the number of outstanding shares and $P_{0,1,2}$ represents the share price at each subsequent moment in time.

At time T_1 the balance sheet of the bank drops to \$965 due to asset erosion. Immediately the capital ratio is affected and drops below the minimum level. Usually the bank would be forced to go to the capital

Assets	Liabilities		Assets	Liabilities		Assets	Liabilities	
1,000	Deposits	880	965	Deposits	880	965	Deposits	880
	Special RC	40		Special RC	40		Special RC	7.8
	Equity	80		Equity	45		Equity	7.2

Observation T_0	Observation T_1	Observation T_2
$N = 20$ $P_0 = \$4$	$N = 20$ $P_1 = \$2.25$	$N = 34.31$ $P_2 = \$2.25$

FIGURE 5.1 Evolution of a Bank's Balance Sheet and Special RC Trigger/Conversion

market and try to raise additional Tier 1 capital, but in this case the SRC kicks in and part of it ($32.2) is converted into equity, which action repairs the bank's capital ratio.

Note that compared to a classic RC bond, the investor does not lose money at the moment of conversion. With an RC the investor generally loses value on the investment because the conversion will only take place when the share price is below the strike price. With an SRC this is not the case, at least at the moment of conversion. In theory the investor could sell the number of shares it is allocated at the conversion share price (if still available) and buy back $27.6 of SRCs. However, in the event of such a triggering the bond price of the SRC would probably also have changed, because we expect that the trigger event would have a negative impact on the CDS spread of the bank, which would be reflected in the price of the SRC, if perhaps only temporarily.

In his paper, Flannery made the assumption that any new SRC bonds subsequently issued could carry the same price as before—that is, they would not need to incorporate a larger default risk premium. The authors are not sure this would be the case; the market would for the time being associate a higher risk with this bank, and new SRCs would most likely have to be issued at a higher yield. The authors' view is that from the moment the capital ratio drops below the minimum level and the conversion is automatically triggered, speculation will arise in the market on the quality of the bank's assets, which in turn will have a negative effect on its credit spread.

The tenor of newly issued SRCs can in theory at least be shorter than classic bank subordinated debt, which is usually issued at medium- and long-dated maturities in order to be accepted as regulatory capital. This is the only way to protect senior debt holders from bankruptcy. SRCs would protect senior debt holders by converting their debt into equity. The protection is in place as long as the maturity of the SRC is much longer than the conversion interval. For SRCs, then, this depends upon the frequency of the conversion intervals. The authors share Flannery's view that a maturity of two years would be sufficient for the SRC if the conversion periods are set (for example) every month. The fact that the bond would be shorter dated than typical bank subordinated bonds would benefit its liquidity in the secondary market, and would also enforce a kind of financial management discipline on the bank, because it would be looking to refinance the SRCs at fairly short regular time periods.

One final issue concerning SRCs is the parameter level that should be set as the appropriate trigger. There is the choice between monitoring the daily market stock price and looking at the book value to determine the capital ratio. Both have their advantages, but for the authors the observation of the market stock price is the more advantageous. Book values can be manipulated by creative accounting techniques and it not uncommon for them to reflect an overly optimistic picture of a bank.

Of course a market stock price might not reflect its true value, either, in the case of distress, but should at least reflect a more realistic picture because of the lemming-like behavior of investors, who will be quick to sell if there is any perceived distress for the bank or in the market. When this happens, it is perhaps better to run the risk of becoming overcapitalized rather than remain viewed as being undercapitalized. If, following a crisis, it appears that the bank is indeed overcapitalized, then it would always be straightforward to return excess capital to the shareholders, via extra dividends or a share buy-back program. A situation of undercapitalization is more dangerous than overcapitalization, with the potential of the government's needing to bail out the bank.

Furthermore, if one bases the trigger event on the stock price, daily price volatility issues can be addressed by taking instead the average price over, say, one week. This also creates a protection against any market manipulation, as it is difficult to manipulate share prices over a prolonged period of time.

Pricing an SRC bond presents more complexity than a classic RC. With an RC the coupon is determined by the premium generated from a reversed knock-in put option that is sold embedded in the bond. For an SRC there are three parameters that determine the value of the bond coupon:

1. The level of (swap) interest rates.
2. The price of the credit default swap (CDS) for subordinated debt of the issuer on that particular maturity.
3. The price of the embedded option, similar to a classic RC.

The major problem for an SRC, however, is the uncertainty of when the option is going to be exercised and at what strike level. One cannot determine up front when the bank's balance sheet is going to drop below the minimum capital ratio level, and as a consequence one does not know at what level the market share price of the issuing bank will be.

This means the embedded option in the SRC will follow a path-dependent road. The end value will depend upon the value of the underlying not only at expiry but also at previous points in time. In other words, the value of the option depends upon the path it undertakes during the lifetime of the option. These options fall under the category of Asian options, and more specifically in this case look-back Asian options.[6]

Look-back options are also path-dependent and their payoff depends upon the maximum or minimum (depending whether it is a call or a put)

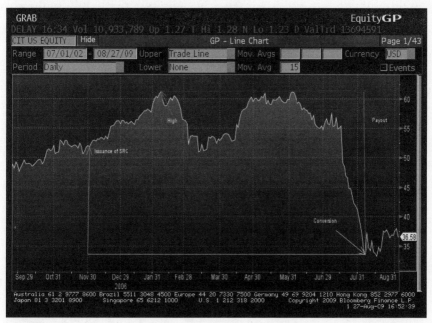

FIGURE 5.2   Payoff Schedule of Floating Strike Put Option
Source: © Bloomberg Finance L.P. All rights reserved. Used with permission.

asset price over the life of the option. As its name suggests, the holder of the look-back can look back over time to determine the payoff.

Look-back options offer the choice between a fixed strike price and a floating strike, and it is the latter that would suit perfectly an SRC structure, in giving an indication of the price of the embedded option as a hedging tool for the issuer. The floating-strike put (FSP) feature will give the issuer the right to sell its underlying stock at the highest price that was observed during the lifetime of the option. This will be a hedge for the issuer to compensate the coupon he needs to pay out on the bond (see Figure 5.2).

The payout value of this option would be:

$$P_T = Max\left[\max_{0<t<T}(S_t) - S_T, 0 \right]$$

where

S is the strike price from time t to maturity time T

A feature of the FSP option is that it can never be out-of-the-money, which as a result will automatically mean that this type of option will be more expensive than a plain-vanilla put option. This also results in a higher coupon and as such a yield pick-up for the investor. Furthermore, the FSP option will have to be of an American type, as the exact moment when the bank's balance sheet value or capital ratio might drop below the required capital ratio is uncertain.

To determine the value of an American-style FSP, one needs to determine the value of a European FSP. The value of the American feature is the sum of the European option value plus a premium for early exercise.

Goldman, Sosin, and Gatto (1979) determined the value of a European FSP based upon the standard Black-Scholes model, as follows:[7]

$$P_E(t, R; T, \theta) = S_{max} e^{-rT} N(b_2) - S e^{-qT} N(-b_1)$$
$$+ S e^{-rT} \frac{\sigma^2}{2(r-q)} \left[- \left(\frac{S}{S_{max}} \right)^{\frac{2(r-q)}{\sigma^2}} N \left(b_1 + \frac{2(r-q)}{\sigma} \sqrt{T} \right) + e^{-qT} N(b_1) \right]$$

where

S = price of stock
q = dividend
r = risk-free rate
T = expiry
t = conversion point
θ = moneyness coefficient
σ = standard deviation or volatility
N = standard normal distribution function

$$b_1 = \frac{\ln \left(\frac{S_{max}}{S} \right) + (q - r + 0.5 \sigma^2) T}{\sigma \sqrt{T}}$$

$$b_2 = b_1 - \sigma \sqrt{T}$$

The American FSP value, therefore, according to Lai and Lim (2004), would be:[8]

$$P_A(t, R) = P_E(t, R; T, \theta) + r \int_t^T e^{-q(r-t)} \varepsilon \left[\gamma - \theta \bar{R}(\tau) \right] F_\varepsilon (R, \bar{R}(\tau), \tau - t) d\tau$$
$$+ r \int_t^T \theta \bar{R}(\tau) P_E(t, R; \tau, \bar{R}(\tau)^{-1}) d\tau$$

where

τ = $T - t$
R = S_{max} / S
$\bar{R}(\tau)$ = the optimal stopping boundary at time τ

$$\gamma = q/r$$

$$F_\in(v, w, \tau) = N\left(-\in\left(d(v, \tau) - \left(\sigma\sqrt{\tau}\right)^{-1}\ln w\right)\right)$$

$$+ w^{2\mu} N\left(\in\left(d(v, \tau) + \left(\sigma\sqrt{\tau}\right)^{-1}\ln w\right)\right)$$

$$d(v, \tau) = \left(\sigma\sqrt{\tau}\right)^{-1}\ln v + \mu\sigma\sqrt{\tau}$$

$$\mu = \gamma p - \rho - 0.5$$

$$\rho = r/\sigma^2$$

The sum of the premium of the option spread out over the lifetime of the bond, which the investor is actually shorting, and the subordinated debt level of the issuer will give a good indication of where the coupon of the SRC can be issued over swap rate levels. In the event of conversion, the issuer recoups this value due to the payout of the look-back option which it buys as a hedge.

We conclude then that an SRC-type capital instrument has considerable merit as a financial shock absorber in times of economic downturn. Whether it would have achieved its purpose sufficiently during the 2008 bank crisis is still doubtful, however, as the leverage ratios of banks had become too high to be able to absorb that kind of shock. In other words, the experience of 2008 is also a call for regulatory authorities to take into account leverage levels at banks and legislate accordingly to limit them.

CHAPTER 6

Economic Theories under Attack

A number of economic theories, such as the portfolio diversification theory of Harry Markowitz and the efficient market hypothesis (EMH) of Eugene Fama, were the subject of criticism during and after the financial crisis of 2007–2009. In essence these criticisms were not new: The models had been the subject of debate in academic circles from virtually their publication date. However, the crisis brought the debate out of academia and into the world of practitioners.

In this chapter we review this criticism, as a prelude to offering our own recommendations for investment managers in Part Two of this book.

A BELIEF IN FREE AND SELF-ADJUSTING MARKETS

After the fall of the Iron Curtain in 1989, certain intellectuals used the victory of capitalism over communism as ammunition to claim that the free market would be robust enough to self-regulate financial markets.

This chapter is not a revolt against capitalism. Far from it. There is no doubt that this economic model has proven its merits over and over again (witness examples such as the improved prosperity and social development in countries that had switched from centrally planned economies to free market economies, ranging from India and Tanzania to China and Vietnam) and is a far superior methodology when compared to communism (at least the forms of communism we have experienced until now). There seems to be no better model available in optimizing the distribution of goods and services, creating wealth, and raising living standards, when measured by typical economic metrics.

Martin Wolf and Paul Krugman, who are also quoted in this book, have described perfectly the catastrophic consequences of blunt interventions in a free market process, for countries such as Mexico, Argentina, Thailand, and Indonesia, to name a few.[1] Normally, interventions of central banks of the major developed nations are neither considered to be blunt nor hampering the correctness of the EMH.

Nevertheless there was a dogmatic belief, fostered during the Reagan and Thatcher administrations in the United States and United Kingdom during the 1980s, that markets were efficient enough to take care of their own problems, and certainly that as far as possible governments should not intervene in the market process. Thus *laissez-faire* capitalism was reintroduced into the world, often called the *Anglo-Saxon* economic model. The economic advisers of both President Ronald Reagan and Prime Minister Margaret Thatcher were fervent supporters of this economic thinking. After the fall of the Berlin Wall, this thinking was raised to a higher level and globalization emerged as a result.

In Chapter 1 we described how globalization made the financial industry more interconnected and created a large volume of liquidity.[2] It puzzled U.S. Federal Reserve Chairman Alan Greenspan why long-term interest rates did not rise in accordance with the Federal Reserve's monetary policy. It is possible that globalization has changed the validity of the economic theories that were developed during the 1950s and 1960s, when markets were completely different compared to now.

Between 1950 and the late 1980s financial markets experienced a number of asset bubbles and crashes. It is not a coincidence that from the 1990s onward, the frequency of bubbles increased, as shown in Table 1.2.

When Eugene Fama proposed the EMH in the 1960s, it triggered an instant debate between market practitioners and academics. The core philosophy of the EMH is that all information is priced into every asset at each moment of time and therefore it is impossible to create a portfolio that would outperform a randomly chosen portfolio with an equal risk profile. Only by adding additional risk can one beat the market.

The theory seems to undermine itself: If it were possible to beat the market by adding more risk, this implies that there are periods of moving in and out of assets where, at inception, the full upside is not priced in, and when this materializes one moves out of the asset. However, this means that at inception this asset would have been mispriced and thus, by definition, not all information is embedded in the price.[3]

The EMH continues by arguing that even if one could perform better than a randomly chosen portfolio, it would be impossible to do this consistently on an individual basis. As a consequence, the theory concludes that markets are not predictable, and this makes them ultimately efficient.

Therefore the fact that markets are not predictable seems to mean that markets are efficient.[4] If markets are unpredictable, one cannot beat the market, because there is no possible upside in hand-picking assets: All assets are correctly priced at all times.

Theory and Practice on a Collision Course

We believe that this thesis has damaged the financial industry over time. A failure of academic belief in this theory arose in 1998 when the hedge fund Long Term Capital Management (LTCM) collapsed under the weight of its excessively leveraged positions. The fund's managers believed that they were smarter than the market, backed by their undoubtedly impressive academic track record.

One particular anecdote concerning LTCM, quoted in Lowenstein (2000) reflects its beliefs. One of the founders of the fund, Myron Scholes, was attending a client meeting during which an investor raised doubts about the advertised strategy of the fund. Mr. Scholes, with a certain amount of irritation, snapped at the client, "The fund will succeed because of fools like you." Strongly believing in the EMH, LTCM managers were convinced they could take advantage of the inefficiencies of the market. What LTCM did not realize was that the market was actually taking advantage of LTCM's own inefficiencies.[5] The mistake the fund managers made was that they believed in a mathematical modeling approach of financial markets, which is not always accurate—it is particularly inefficient in allowing for outlier events—and is actually a completely different subject.

Notwithstanding the LTCM experience, the trend in approaching markets more scientifically continued, to the point where bank dealing rooms included mathematicians, physicists, and other financial engineers. In the main these individuals, the so-called *quants*, have a similar background and they invariably all use the same models, mathematical approaches that originated in statistical physics.

Many quants use a methodology known as the ARCH/GARCH models, which are techniques that observe a series of historical data and use this to make expectations about future volatility, assuming a certain state of the economy. This means that data from the past has embedded information that sets an expected value in the future. Similarly in option pricing theory, such a historic observation window is used and market shocks are typically not incorporated, due to the statistical nature of the normal distribution.

A similar approach was used by the credit rating agencies. These firms implicitly assumed that real estate prices could never fall on a national scale, simply because statistical evidence suggested this was so. Economic shocks or changes in economic states were typically ignored, since random behavior can be used to anticipate future states. If enough market participants ignore the same states of the world, the market price is automatically incomplete; thus not all information is priced in, and hence markets are not efficient.[6]

The danger is, however, and this came to the surface during the financial crash of 2007–2009, that if every derivative trader is using the same model, everybody is going to take the same price (which is produced by the model) for granted. The issue here is that at the moment the market drops out of the comfort zone or interval of what the model is used to, one is faced with a substantial systemic risk.

The analogy we make has been quoted in earlier literature. As long as all the cars on the highway are driving at 100 mph, there is nothing wrong, but as soon as one of them has to stop, it causes serious disruption.

The Issue of Rationality

The ARCH/GARCH methodology is paradoxical to what the EMH proclaims, as the theory doubts the predicting power of markets. Modifications of GARCH exist that try to incorporate market shocks. For instance, another technique used in econometrics is the Kalman filter, which is a recursive filter, also referred to as a prediction filter in physics. The name identifies the contradiction with the EMH.[7] In this we agree. However, to us there is a major difference between predictability and being rational. If every market participant was rational then it would not make sense to deviate from the benchmark, in which case secondary market volumes would be zero.

This assumption of rationality is therefore also a big weakness in the theory. Apart from theoretical work—such as Kahneman suggesting that rationality of investors is doubtful as rational decision making is often not feasible due to the restricted resources each individual has available—there is also empirical evidence of irrationality.[8] First of all, if markets were populated only by rational investors, there would never be any bubbles, and Table 1.2 proves this to the contrary. Another example of irrationality can be detected with shares of holding companies. It can be observed that shares of holding companies often trade at a lower price than the capitalized amount of cash these holdings have on their accounts. Other examples of anomalies can be found in the credit market—for example, the phenomenon of negative-basis trade opportunities, when the spread in the credit default swap (CDS) of the underlying issuer is lower than the spread of the bond itself in the cash market.

The EMH continues by saying that it is possible to outperform the index only by adding additional risk. Inside information is illegal, which leaves only one exit to the investor: to start predicting the future.

It is exactly this that dominates the market. There is an obsession with forecasting in the financial industry. During the earnings reporting season, bank research analysts focus on company results and whether these will miss or beat analyst estimates. Another example is the nervousness that precedes the release of major economic data. These attitudes are by no means the sole responsibility of the EMH. To outperform the market, one has to be capable of selecting mispriced assets and waiting for the market to become efficient again, thereby eliminating these mismatches. However, in an efficient market the mispricing is not supposed to occur in the first place.

Other Anomalies

There are further problems with the EMH. It has a big influence on the impact of risk management and the concept of risk. Risk is measured via the standard deviation of volatility, which is also used in the value at risk (VaR) measurement methodology. VaR suffers from the same problems as the pricing models of bank quantitative analysts. It makes projections based on what happened in the past, which ultimately delivers a false sense of security.

Intuitively, the idea of measuring risk based upon volatility creates mixed feelings. It is viable to argue that investors are more concerned about downside volatility than upward moves. However, the EMH and the theories that came thereafter value these two types of volatility in equal measure.

Furthermore, the concept of risk in the EMH carries a contradiction. John Mauldin, the investment manager and writer, compared the return and risk between growth stocks and value stocks. The risk expressed in terms of volatility is higher for growth stocks than it is for value stocks. This is not an issue as growth stocks are more venture-capital-related and intuitively one would expect that they represent higher risk. Nevertheless, in Mauldin's study it transpires that the return on value stocks is higher than that on growth stocks.[9] This is a fundamental contradiction of the EMH, which argues that additional risk should be rewarded by the market with higher returns.[10] This is shown in Figures 6.1 and 6.2.

Much earlier, J. Michael Murphy had reached a similar conclusion, as reported in a 1977 paper on the efficiency of markets, in which he argued that ". . . there is not necessarily any stable relationship between risk and return, and . . . there often may be virtually no relationship between return achieved and risk taken."[11]

Another reminder of this is the fact that the financial crisis of 2007–2009 started with the collapse of two money market funds managed sby BNP Paribas in the summer of 2007. This had been triggered by an increased distrust by investors in asset-backed commercial paper, which

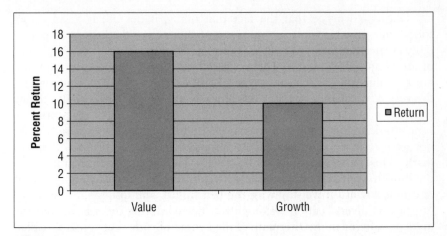

FIGURE 6.1   Return Profile of Growth versus Value Stocks
Source: John Mauldin, "Six impossible things before breakfast," Weekly Newsletter, August 7, 2009.

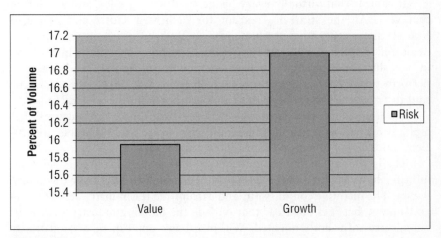

FIGURE 6.2   Risk Profile of Growth versus Value Stocks
Source: John Mauldin, "Six impossible things before breakfast," Weekly Newsletter, August 7, 2009.

were suspected of investing in risky assets. Once again, if the EMH applies in reality, then commercial paper and other money market instruments should represent lower risk assets than equities. As the EMH discourages an investor from deviating from the benchmark, it has a strong influence on how the financial industry is obsessed with benchmark assessment unless, as mentioned earlier, one adds new risks.

One could argue that the fact that many, if not all, large investors follow the same principle increases the inefficiency of the market. It potentially creates bubbles, since there is too much money chasing the same type of assets and all institutions have virtually the same type of portfolio and are all vulnerable to the same type of risk. If this type of risk submerges, the very scale of these institutions tends to transform a potentially minor risk into a major event due to the same end reaction of all investors.[12] A benchmarking approach becomes a self-fulfilling prophecy as investors do not want to jeopardize their career prospects and move outside the benchmark. This, however, is in contrast with the hedge fund community. A question to ask then is, if markets are efficient, should we simply accept that in a downturn we stay with the benchmark and lose money anyway?

Just as diversification was highly criticized during the sell-off that the markets suffered in the aftermath of the Lehman Brothers collapse, so-called *alpha* was criticized as well. Consider Table 6.1, which shows the performance of the hedge fund industry in the midst of the crisis, as at the end of 2008.

It is clear that virtually every hedge fund manager lost money during that year. All the strategies (except for dedicated shorts and managed futures) show a negative performance for 2008. One can argue that both dedicated shorts and managed futures are pure directional plays, like betting in a casino, and anticipate a negative downturn, and so would always perform positively in the environment of 2008. Such strategies cannot be said to represent the application of modern portfolio theory (MPT).

The immediate circumstantial evidence from Table 6.1 suggests that alpha is a myth as well. But this would also suggest that markets are efficient, and we are convinced that this is not the case.

The issue may be that a significant number of people in the hedge fund industry have left the politicized world of banking to start their own companies. The lucrative commissions and earnings in the industry attract many ex-bankers, but it is not clear that outside the banking industry such individuals are sufficiently talented. Within a bank one can be a good trader simply by using the flow stream of the franchise, but there is a huge difference between doing that and investing on one's own with a blank sheet and turning new trades into profitable investments.

It may also be that it is more a case of doing one's homework properly, by asking the proper questions instead of attempting to predict the future. Those who succeed in doing so will indeed ultimately outperform their competitors. This means that the investor has to take a directional view, although not necessarily any additional risk. However, predicting the future using directional plays is not necessarily what being an effective investor is about.

TABLE 6.1 Credit Suisse/Tremont Hedge Fund Index Performance

	Index Value		Return		YTD
	Dec-08	Nov-08	Dec-08	Nov-08	
Credit Suisse/Tremont Hedge Fund Index	351.08	351.2	−0.03%	−4.15%	−19.07%
Convertible Arbitrage	221.62	223.82	−0.98%	−1.88%	−31.59%
Dedicated Short Bias	88.94	90.46	−1.68%	3.04%	14.87%
Emerging Markets	264.49	263.92	0.22%	−1.87%	−30.41%
Equity Market Neutral	225.47	224.54	0.41%	−40.85%	−40.32%
Event Driven	395.52	400.56	−1.26%	−3.21%	−17.74%
Distressed	452.18	463.96	−2.54%	−5.00%	−20.48%
Multi-Strategy	371.03	372.86	−0.49%	−2.17%	−16.25%
Risk Arbitrage	277.63	273.26	1.60%	−0.02%	−3.27%
Fixed Income Arbitrage	166.79	168.13	−0.80%	−5.60%	−28.82%
Global Macro	582.69	576.3	1.11%	1.54%	−4.62%
Long/Short Equity	401.98	397.78	1.06%	−1.41%	−19.76%
Managed Futures	284.19	277.61	2.37%	3.22%	18.33%
Multi-Strategy	275.79	280.04	−1.52%	−4.63%	−23.63%

Note: All currencies in USD.
Source: Credit Suisse/Tremont Hedge Fund Index. Reproduced with permission.

The Issue of Volatility

A final issue regarding the risk-volatility approach is the assumption that volatility is constant over time. Skewness of the volatility curve is completely ignored by the EMH. Options traders take this into account on a daily basis. An options trader does not quote the same volatility every day, but rather adjusts prices to take the smile of the volatility curve into account for in-the-money (ITM), out-of-the-money (OTM), or at-the-money (ATM) options.

Figure 6.3 shows the skew of the volatility of a six-month option of XAU versus USD. One can clearly see that the volatility for calls compared to puts is higher and rises for far out-of-the money options. So the assumption of constant volatility is a fundamental weakness of orthodox EMH theory.

There are a few reasons why a volatility curve shows a smile:

- Supply and demand among hedgers and speculators.
- Directional view of the market.
- Implied volatility usually goes up when the spot price moves.
- Exotic options: Market makers use OTM options to statically hedge exotic risk, which means that they are unwilling to short OTM options.

Thus a reality of the marketplace, the behavior of options traders when setting prices, shows that the theoretical approach of the EMH is not followed in practical terms by market practitioners.

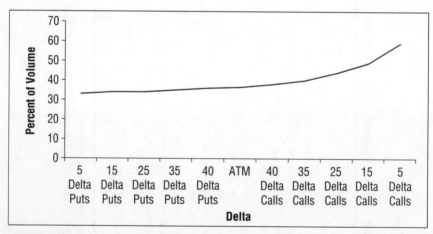

FIGURE 6.3 XAU/USD Volatility Smile
Data source: Bloomberg.

MODIGLIANI AND MILLER

In this book we already highlighted the issue of leverage, which was a contributory factor behind the banking crisis in 2008. But this addiction to debt had its origin in another economic theory that was groundbreaking for corporate finance: Modigliani and Miller's capital cost model or theorem.

The basics of this theory are that a firm's capital structure has no ultimate relevance for a company. Whether it is by holding equity or issuing debt, it does not really matter. The cost of capital remains unchanged when a corporation raises its financial leverage.[13] Or to quote Modigliani and Miller (MM):

> *With well-functioning markets (and neutral taxes) and rational investors, who can "undo" the corporate financial structure by holding positive or negative amounts of debt, the market value of the firm—debt plus equity—depends only on the income stream generated by its assets. It follows, in particular, that the value of the firm should not be affected by the share of debt in its financial structure or by what will be done with the returns—paid out as dividends or reinvested (profitably).*[14]

The theory ignores the increased risk of default that arises when a company is burdened with excess debt. During the banking crisis in 2007–2009, many banks (we ignore corporations at this point) were on the verge of collapse due to the enormous leverage that they had built up over the years. This was shown earlier in Chapter 3.

Although MM's original theory was written in 1958 and updated in 1961 and 1963, it was still based on the same assumptions as the EMH—that is, the functioning of perfect markets populated with rational investors. The MM theory is perhaps a minor causal factor so we downplay it as a driver of the 2008 crash. Leverage built up over time was at least as much a result of the low price of credit risk and the excess supply of cheap funding. But the former issue reflects a shortcoming of the EMH, which struggles with the definition of risk.

MARKOWITZ AND DIVERSIFICATION TESTED

Earlier we discussed the issue of alpha and diversification. This brings us to another groundbreaking theory, the modern portfolio theory (MPT) of Markowitz.[15]

The main idea behind MPT is that when investing, one should always try to diversify the investment over a wide range of different assets, to avoid putting all one's eggs in the same basket, so to speak. Although this is indeed common sense, nevertheless the assumptions on which MPT is based are flawed as well. Similarly to the EMH, MPT assumes that all investors act rationally and that markets are efficient. The issues surrounding these two assumptions have already been discussed.

To come to an optimal diversified portfolio, MPT uses statistical tools such as correlation to measure the effect diversification can have on the return of a portfolio. The rule of thumb here is that the lower the correlation among several assets in the portfolio, the lower the probability that they will move in the same direction.

Furthermore, MPT argues that instead of creating a portfolio by picking out individual stocks, one should keep the portfolio as a whole as an objective. This means that one should focus on the risk/reward potential of the portfolio in total, instead of measuring each security separately. It is therefore important to make a distinction among several asset classes, such as equities, bonds, commodities, currencies, and so on.

Certainly it is logical when Markowitz theory states that asset value correlation needs to be as low as possible in order to optimize return. The major problem, however, is how to apply this in practice.

During the buildup to the crash and crisis of 2007–2009, many investors were putting on similar trades such as the yen carry trade. In a *carry trade* one borrows in a low-interest-rate currency and invests this in a high-yielding currency. We would also call a trade that exploits the steepness of the yield curve, borrowing at the short end of the curve and investing in longer-dated maturities, a carry trade.

Many market participants, including the U.S. government, corporations, banks, and hedge funds, put similar such trades on their books. The U.S. government, by keeping the majority of its debt at as short a maturity as possible, could be said to be undertaking a kind of carry trade. U.S. corporations issued much short-term debt to finance acquisitions. The banking industry mismatched its asset-liability management (ALM) via the shadow banking system. The consumer was financing house purchases via mortgage products that were based on low initial short-term rates.

On paper one could argue that each of these participants was investing in different assets, which might each show statistically low correlation with each other. This is a valid point—however, it was only a partial diversification that was achieved because each market participant took too few truly safe assets onto its books. In practice, every investor had a false sense of security by thinking it had a good diversified portfolio among several types of risky assets. Unfortunately, when risk aversion strikes, a rush toward safe assets will demonstrate that the correlation among these different risky assets is far higher than previously thought.

Due to leverage, many investment portfolios were overloaded with risky assets, which showed a correlation of virtually unity when the deleveraging process began. This was what happened in the aftermath of the Lehman collapse. (Incidentally, the economist Hyman Minsky had predicted such an event two decades before.) This also explains Figure 6.3, where almost every hedge fund, although each is managed within a different strategy and/or asset class, showed negative performance at the end of 2008. Only those funds that took a directional view to short the market—akin to a straight gambler's punt—showed positive returns.

The mutual fund industry, which lost between 40 and 50 percent in value during the crisis, depending on which industry the funds had exposure to, was hit severely. This demonstrates how funds can fall victim to the results of following the EMH, which promotes benchmark investing.

Professor Jonathan Lewellen of Dartmouth Business School arrived at an interesting conclusion regarding benchmark investing and diversification. Lewellen analyzed the performance of institutional equity portfolios during 1980–2007 and concluded that institutional investors were not very talented when it came to picking stocks and demonstrating outperformance. The vast majority of investors are simply holding what is called the market portfolio. As a consequence, the correlation of the portfolios held by U.S. institutional investors came out at 99.8 percent—in other words, unity. Furthermore, institutional investors apparently do not really attempt to differentiate themselves from the benchmark. They appear to focus more on idiosyncratic returns, and less frequently exploit anomalies.[16]

The latter one might expect among hedge fund investors, who commonly try to deviate from the market. More importantly, however, this uniform behavior puts a question mark against the justification of fees that are charged by conventional asset managers.

Lewellen's findings confirm the false sense of security achieved by holding a so-called diversified portfolio, and explain why many portfolios are vulnerable during a market downturn. A big failing is a lack of appreciation of the concept of risk. Nassim Taleb expressed this in the following terms during an interview with McKinsey in 2008:

> We learn from crisis to crisis that MPT has the empirical and scientific validity of astrology, without the aesthetics. . . . Portfolio theory simply doesn't work. It uses metrics like variance to describe risk, while most real risk comes from a single observation, so variance is a volatility that doesn't really describe the risk. It's very foolish to use variance.[17]

It does appear that at best the EMH, MPT, and MM are contradictory to what actually occurs in the real economy, if we observe the events of the past three decades. At worst, the theories bear some not inconsiderable responsibility for the creation of the recent crises.

MINSKY ONCE AGAIN

In light of the preceding consideration, it behooves academics to temper the power of these theories, when teaching them to their students, and perhaps to highlight the work of another economist: Hyman Minsky.

Where Eugene Fama and others failed to justify the existence of economic bubbles, Minsky succeeds in explaining that economic instability is inherent to our financial system. This is mainly due to the fact that our economy and the financing of asset purchases are driven by debt.

The economy moves systematically through three business cycles which are characterized by hedge, then speculative, and ultimately a Ponzi-style finance regime.[18]

At the first stage, the cash flows generated by the purchased asset will be more than enough to fulfill the liability of cash payments. This is usually a period just after the burst of a bubble. Financiers are extremely cautious and debt issuance is rather low. This is how the economic landscape looked like in 2009 as banks still went through a deleveraging process.

A second phase is when the cash flows of the financed asset will not be enough to offset the cash payment liabilities, at least not in the short term. However, over a longer period of time, the financier believes the asset will generate enough cash flows to offset these liabilities. Therefore the possibility of rolling over debt is foreseen. In the most recent crisis, the period that best represents this phase is 2003–2004.

In the third and last phase there is a state resembling euphoria, during which bank lending standards are so loose that the likelihood of repayment is low, and continuous refinancing and increasing debt are a necessity. At this stage one is extremely vulnerable to any change in the interest cost structure—for example, a widening of credit spreads, or an interruption in the cash flows generated by the purchased asset. Usually a series of credit events or bankruptcies is necessary to return to phase one or two. The recent period that best describes this phase of the cycle would be 2006–2007.

These are the basics of Minksy's financial instability hypothesis (FIH), which stands in stark contrast to the EMH and also to the neoclassical school which believes in a perfect equilibrium. To quote from Minsky:

TABLE 6.2 Overview of Bubbles in History

Period	Bubble
1637	Tulip crisis
1720	South Sea Company crisis
1720	Mississippi Company crisis
1840	Railway hysteria
1927	Florida real estate bubble
1929	Stock market bubble
1966	U.S. credit crunch
1972	U.S. banking crisis
1980–1982	U.S. savings and loan crisis
1982	Latin America crisis
1987	Stock market bubble
1988	Japan bubble
1997	Asian crisis
1998	Russian crisis
2000	Dot-com bubble
2001	Argentina crisis
2007–2008	Great credit crisis

The fundamental propositions of the FIH are:

- *Capitalistic market mechanisms cannot lead to a sustained stable price, full employment equilibrium.*
- *Serious business cycles are due to financial attributes that are essential to capitalism.*[19]

Minsky recognizes that an accumulation of debt via the use of leverage has contributed to these cycles. When we look at the list of bubbles humankind has experienced over time, those after World War II were characterized by an overload of debt. (See Table 6.2.)

LESSONS TO BE LEARNED BY CENTRAL BANKS

This brings us back to the discussion regarding central banks. Professor Minsky, long before the authors of this book, reached the same conclusions that we did on the responsibilities of central banks when the issue of cooling down monetary expansion after a period of expansion comes to the fore. Banks actually are the driving force behind monetary interventions, but these come often too late, as shown in Figure 6.4.

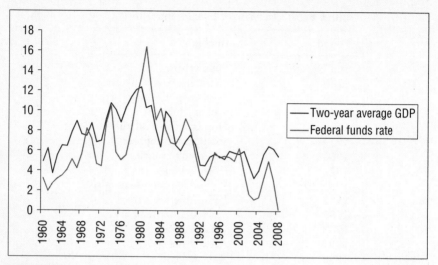

FIGURE 6.4   U.S. Two-Year Nominal GDP Growth versus Federal Funds Rate 1960–2008
Data source: Bloomberg.

Central banks focus overmuch on inflation targeting and not enough on asset price developments, while their impact on changing the money supply is rather limited. Despite this fact, central banks still use interest rates to steer the demand side. When demand is impaired, interest rates will be lowered, and vice versa. It is therefore key to get the timing right as to exactly when to withdraw monetary stimuli. If not, it is the beginning of another bubble.

This is what happened when the Federal Reserve was dealing with the aftermath of the dot-com bubble and the 9/11 events. The Fed was evidently late in hiking rates and stopping an inflating housing bubble. As Gerald O'Driscoll Jr., a former adviser of the Federal Reserve Bank of Dallas, argues: ". . . a continued bias against inflation will produce a continued bias upward in price inflation."[20]

The mismatch in timing of monetary rate policy versus economic growth is something central banks always struggle with. If one compares the change in the federal funds rate with the average growth rate in terms of GDP during the previous two years, one gets a clear view of the overshooting of monetary policy of the Fed. (See Figure 6.4.)

Figure 6.4 shows the recent crisis was not a one-off incident. In 1974 the Fed cut rates aggressively from 10.5 percent to 5 percent over a period of two years. In the second year, though, the economy was already taking off again and the Fed wanted to catch up on its previous monetary easing, which contributed to the banking crisis of the 1980s. The central bank's intervention can almost be compared with a pendulum that goes from one extreme to another.

Given the limited amount of success in controlling the money supply, putting caps on the use of leverage might hold the key to reducing the risk of sharp economic downturns. Or, to quote Minsky once again:

> *To control the disruptive influence that emanates from banking, it is necessary to set limits upon permissible leverage ratios and to constrain the growth of bank equity to a rate that is compatible with noninflationary economic growth. This principle should guide policy, but in an economy in which new financial usages and institutions appear in response to profit opportunities, it is a principle that is much easier to state than to translate in practice.*[21]

This suggests that Minsky was ahead of his time. However, the difficulty of maintaining this balancing act in practice becomes clear when looking at the following conundrum.

Financial institutions are pushed toward financial innovation when interest rates are high. This enables them to create cheap money alternatives. However, we have seen that what took place before the outbreak of the financial crisis was exactly the opposite. After the previous bubble (the dot-com bubble), the market emerged into a period of what was a historical low-interest-rate environment.

The financial innovations that took place then were certainly of a technically high standard. During 2002–2007 the low risk premium was a driving force for financial innovation, as investors sought to raise extra yield in an environment of tightening credit spreads. As a consequence, there is a constant tension field between the liability and asset sides of a bank, with a push for innovation, which automatically creates cycles that put central banks to the test. Furthermore, the risk premium that is increasing and decreasing in line with these cycles cannot be controlled by the monetary authorities, either.

At the time of this writing, we are still in an environment where risk premiums are too low, due to global imbalances. There remain excess funds, coming from the Asian and oil-exporting countries, chasing a paucity of assets. This in turn pushes yields further down, which then forces investors to use leverage. Therefore it is challenging if not impossible to avoid a next crisis, despite new regulation being put in place.

It will also be a delicate exercise to put the appropriate regulation in place, because in the aftermath of the recession legislators respond to an environment of populism. The risk remains that the wrong regulation will be implemented. For example at the time of this writing, the U.S.

government was considering limiting the size of financial institutions by restricting their activities. In Chapter 3 on too-big-to-fail, we already mentioned that this type of measure has some merit as a solution to handle the risk of large banks. However, it is not necessarily a panacea. The objective would be that banks could no longer invest in or sponsor hedge funds and private equity, and/or be involved in proprietary trading. A second proposal was to limit consolidation with broader limits on the market share of liabilities that any financial institution can hold.

The first proposal carries the risk of acting as a brake on the efficient functioning of the financial markets. The objective of the government is laudable, that taxpayers' money should not be used again to bail out banks for speculative purposes and reduce volatile markets. However, this type of reform endangers the liquidity of the market, which ultimately will raise volatility. Therefore if this type of regulation is put in place it would be counterproductive. Prohibiting banks to be involved in these types of market activities will make markets even less efficient and increase the danger of blowing up bubbles even further because, due to a lack of market activity, the market will be driven into one direction.

CONCLUSION

It would not be accurate to say that the EMH, portfolio theory, and the related academic theories triggered the financial crisis, but there is a strong case to be made that these theories were highly influential in creating a mentality, among legislators and regulators as well as investors, that contributed to the imbalances which ultimately caused the crash.

If it was not clear before the crisis that markets are more irrational than is posited in the EMH, it should certainly be easier to get acquainted with this idea now, after the crisis. As important, the financial industry should become more critical about the added value of financial engineering. Mike Gelband of Lehman Brothers once stated, we believe correctly, that "one cannot model human behavior with mathematics."[22] Unfortunately, this is precisely what many people in the financial industry are still doing.

There is no doubt that models can work in certain situations or market environments, but a blind belief in their accuracy, even subconsciously, is naïve if not dangerous. There will always come a time when lemming-like behavior will challenge these models. To this extent we believe there is an important lesson to be learned for the academic world as well. Business schools and economic graduate programs should focus as much on behavioral finance as on the EMH. This should include the research and findings of Minsky.

TWO

New Models for Banking and Investment

In Part One we reviewed the many features and contributory factors of the financial crash of 2007–2009. We saw that a significant number of these causal factors had been building over a period of time and would require both concerted, direct action as well as another period of time to elapse before they could be unwound, such that they did not remain a potential cause of a future crash. Some of the other causes of the crash were the same ones that have always plagued financial markets, including poor loan origination standards and human nature that feeds on, and drives, an asset bubble.

Given that financial crashes appear to be an inherent part of the economic system, it behooves banks and investors to take steps to mitigate the impact of the next crash. In Part Two, we provide our recommendations on what these steps should be. While not necessarily the full list, or indeed even an exhaustive one, we have reasoned that the measures described here should be part of a logical, dispassionate review of strategy by both banks and investors. We begin with a look at our recommendations for an investment and portfolio strategy, in Chapter 7, before moving on to the suggested new bank business model in Chapters 8 and 9.

CHAPTER 7

Long-Term Sustainable Investment Guidelines

Following any assessment of the causes and impact of the financial crash of 2007–2009, the economic imbalances that are still in place and how markets behaved over the past two and perhaps three decades, it is evident that a review of the principal investment guidelines in use during this period is due.

In Part One we noted the increased frequency of market crises over the past decade. In our view the most recent crisis has sown the seeds of the next crisis, despite new regulation and corporate governance rules now being put in place. A recent study from Reinhart and Rogoff (2008) provides some insight into this subject, and is a notable pointer for a re-evaluation of how investors should approach the markets in the future. The most important principle is that of capital preservation. This reflects the fact that the Western world is faced with an aging population that is going to put ever-increasing pressure on pension funds, government Social Security budgets, and each of us as an individual investor.

The objective of this chapter is certainly not to provide a template for which stocks or bonds one should invest in. As we argued in Chapter 6, an excess of participants in the financial industry focus on micro-forecasting. Of course one needs to take a directional view, but this is overemphasized in the current paradigm. Investing can be undertaken in a more sensible way than blindly picking out certain stocks.

THE INVESTMENT LANDSCAPE AFTER THE CRISIS

The new investment paradigm concentrates on asset rotation. In this approach four major asset classes play a pivotal role in the investment portfolio: interest rates and inflation (as these are closely related), currencies, specified commodities, and emerging markets.

TABLE 7.1   Total Debt as a Percentage of GDP in 2008

Country	2008 Total Debt (percent of GDP)
United Kingdom	469
Japan	459
Spain	342
Switzerland	313
France	308
Italy	298
United States	290
Germany	274
Canada	245
China	159
Brazil	142
India	129
Russia	71

Source: McKinsey, January 2010.

In the first place, one needs to understand what happened during the crash, in order to avoid potential damage to one's future investments. This is a fundamentally different approach to that of predicting, say, whether the iPad will be the next superproduct that will double the stock price at Apple. Taking a macro-level view on finance and economics will assist more long-term, value-added investment decisions, as well as identify the right asset classes.

As illustrated elsewhere in this book, the credit crunch triggered significant deleveraging in the private sector. However, the world has not subsequently become a safer place. The debt buildup among banks and consumers in the period before the 2007 crash has now transferred to the public sector.

Table 7.1 shows that total outstanding debt levels, taking every sector into account (corporations, financials, nonfinancials, households, and governments), are a source for concern in the developed markets, despite the deleveraging that occurred in the financial sector.

A study from McKinsey (2009) suggests that it takes between five and seven years to deleverage after a crash.[1] Using this as a guide and dating the start of the crash in the summer of 2007, this suggests that the process will not be complete until at least 2012. Going forward, this will have a significant impact on economic growth. The same study argues that growth will only start to pick up three to four years after the most recent crash. We illustrate the hypothetical cycle in Figure 7.1.

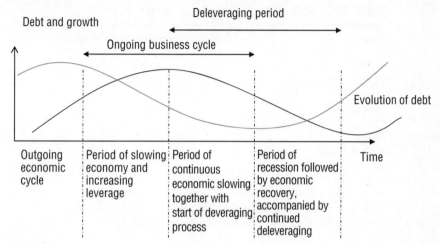

FIGURE 7.1 Deleveraging and Growth Cycle Relationship, Timeline

GOVERNMENT DEBT AND DEMOGRAPHICS

We consider first the state of Western government debt, and the expected future impact of demographic changes.

Government Debt

As we have observed during the latest deleveraging cycle, government debts are growing. This issue exacerbates a problem for certain developed countries whose public finances were becoming unsustainable even before the onset of the crash. In this regard we note Japan, whose economy has been in a deflationary situation for over a decade; the United States; and the southern eurozone countries, which are threatened by a sovereign debt crisis (see Table 7.2).

The fund manager Bill Gross of PIMCO used the analogy of a "ring of fire" for such countries, and placed the respective countries in an illustrative matrix, as shown in Figure 7.2.[2]

This is not an unusual phenomenon. Reinhart and Rogoff (2008) analyzed financial crises and their effects.[3] In their paper they concluded that the aftermath of banking crises is followed by a sharp rise of domestic debt (between 50 and 100 percent), which consequently triggers a high inflation rate and ultimately ends in a series of defaults on outstanding sovereign debt, and sometimes a currency crisis. We note from their study that these

TABLE 7.2   Public Debt as a Percentage of GDP in 2009

Country	2009 Public debt (percent of GDP)
United Kingdom	58.7*
Japan	198.6
Spain	44.2
Switzerland	48.1
France	65.2
Italy	104.3
United States	61.5
Germany	76.4
Canada	60.7

Source: International Monetary Fund (IMF) and Organisation for Economic Co-operation and Development (OECD).

series of events show a cyclical pattern and, more importantly, a high number of defaults and/or restructuring of countries' debts for a prolonged period. Since World War II this period has taken an average of three years. To quote Reinhart and Rogoff,

> . . . *serial default on external debt—that is, repeated sovereign default—is the norm throughout every region in the world, even including Asia and Europe.*[4]

One can argue that they are referring to external debt, and in the current environment countries, as we explained in Chapter 1 on globalization, rely more on domestic debt, which at first sight looks like a safer situation. However, it is naïve to believe that domestic debt would be treated in a subordinated way compared to external debt. Any type of extreme debt buildup has a damaging impact on the economy. This has supporting evidence in history, and among academics there is broad consensus on this view. Hyman Minsky described the phenomenon in detail, as we noted in Chapter 6.

What is most relevant is the total debt level. Every prolonged period of economic downturn has been preceded by a period of excess debt. Table 7.2 and Figure 7.2 suggest that this situation has not changed. Furthermore, the private savings dynamic of a nation can play a shock-absorbing role. There is an unwritten rule that whatever the public sector spends needs to be offset by the private sector, and vice versa. From this perspective both the United States and United Kingdom are in a worrying situation, due to their low savings ratios.

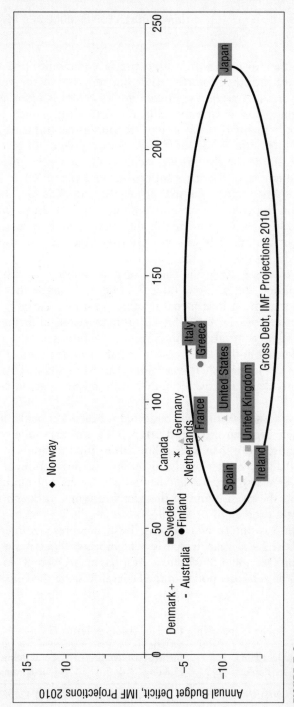

FIGURE 7.2 Sovereign Debt Projections
Source: PIMCO, January 2010, and IMF.

Also important to note is the sharp rise in commodity prices. These are an important indicator for countries that may be on the verge of a sovereign debt crisis. A steep rise in commodity prices is often accompanied by an inflationary environment. In the orthodox manner a rise in inflation is usually met with a rise in interest rates as central banks seek to tackle the rise in prices. While inflation erodes the value of government debt, in the meantime the rise in rates adds to the debt-servicing burden. In the 1980s a number of countries suffered from a vicious circle in which the interest snowball effect caused problems; for example, Italy and Belgium were enveloped in a debt spiral with gearing interest payments. At that time interest rates were at double-digit levels, and so interest payments on the outstanding debt of such countries began to rise at an accelerated level.

The crash of 2007–2009 has placed several countries in this danger, including the United States. From Table 7.2 one could argue that the situation there is not as precarious as that in other countries. Carrying a public debt of 61.5 percent of GDP could be seen as manageable at first sight. The problem arises if we translate this into absolute numbers.

Based on data from the U.S. Treasury Department, the total U.S. public debt outstanding in January 2010 was more than $12 trillion. This amount can be split into debt held by the public intragovernment holdings (see Table 7.3).

The Obama administration has budgeted for an additional cumulative $9 trillion deficit between 2010 and 2019. This will bring the total U.S. national debt, now more than $12 trillion, above $20 trillion.

This rising debt simultaneously increases the proportion of interest rates the U.S. Treasury Department has to pay on its outstanding debt. Table 7.4 shows the rising trend of the past five years, although the data for 2009 shows a drop.

This situation is due to two reasons. First, it represents interest paid till the end of the fiscal year, which is September 2009. For the months October through December 2009 the interest payments were $145 million. Second, due to the zero rate policy of the Federal Reserve the U.S. Treasury

TABLE 7.3   U.S. Public Outstanding Debt in Absolute Terms

Current	Debt Held by Public	Intragovernmental Holdings	Total Public Debt Outstanding
1/28/2010	$7,759,907,274,242.18	$4,514,524,153,795.10	$12,274,431,428,037.20

Source: Bureau of the Public Debt and United States Department of the Treasury.

TABLE 7.4 U.S. Total Interest
Payments on Public Debt

Year	USD
2005	352,350,252,507.90
2006	405,872,109,315.83
2007	429,977,998,108.20
2008	451,154,049,950.63
2009	383,071,060,815.42

Source: Bureau of the Public Debt
and United States Department of the
Treasury.

is saving on its interest payments. So these amounts will rise again as the
U.S. government continues to run such deficits.

This is the core of the problem. U.S. public debt servicing is extremely
vulnerable to a rise in interest rates. One can expect that in the period
after 2010, following a prolonged zero-interest rate policy, interest rates
will be raised and then peak at a higher level. If one assumes that U.S.
interest rates will rise to the average level of the past 40 years, then interest
payments will rise to above $1 trillion annually.

At the end of 2009 the average maturity of U.S. government debt was
around 48 to 50 months. This is the shortest tenor observed since 1983. A
vast majority of debt is concentrated at the short end of the yield curve.
The U.S. Treasury is aware of the risks associated with this fact; for
instance, in 2009 Treasury Secretary Timothy Geithner stated that he would
like to see the average maturity rise to above 70 months.

Demographic Concerns

The large and increasing public debt will have a significant impact on future
economic growth performance globally. If a large part of government revenues (taxes) has to be used in paying interest on outstanding debt, then
there is little room for debt reduction and, even more importantly, for
investment. The latter will be extremely challenging for the Western world,
which is faced with an aging population.

Demographic issues will place social security budgets under pressure.
Population issues cannot be excluded when talking about a new investment
model, because they have an impact on the way we are going to invest.[5]
The aging of the population has a potential accelerating effect on rising

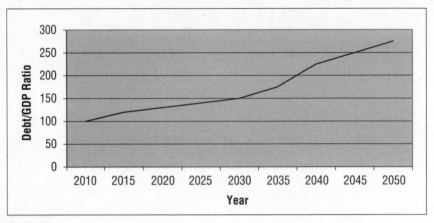

FIGURE 7.3   G20 Economies' Forecasted Government Debt Evolution
Source: IMF, March 2009.

government deficits. To put this into perspective we illustrate with some data, based upon studies by the IMF[6] and Barclays Bank.[7]

Both studies anticipate a rise in government debt of at least 50 percent among the developed G20 countries. From 2030 onward this will accelerate and government debt ratios of 275 percent of GDP are forecast to be seen by 2050 in the West.

Figure 7.3 shows the average picture for the G20 on aggregate. Some countries are in a poorer situation than others. Data from the IMF indicates that Japan and South Korea will experience demographic issues that will pressure their public finances severely. For example, Japan already has government debt of almost 200 percent of GDP. By 2030 an expected additional 190 percent of GDP, at today's numbers, may be added to this debt. Of course this ignores future economic growth levels, which will increase absolute GDP levels. In the case of the United States, the forecast is 40 percent of GDP added to its current government debt level by 2030.

The problem then is that due to the financial crisis, governments' savings that would have covered for this demographic shock have been used to prevent the economy from falling into depression. In essence the reserves that had been built up have disappeared. This would apply to many of the eurozone countries that applied fiscal discipline over a 10-year period to fulfill the terms of the Maastricht Treaty.

There are other countries where the situation is as bad if not worse. In the United States and United Kingdom, reserves have been extinguished. Both economies have strong private pension schemes compared to those in Continental Europe. However, this is no panacea. U.S. and UK household savings rates are low, and poorer than levels in mainland Europe. In the decade 2000–2009 the savings ratio fell to 2 percent and 4 percent, respectively. The savings rate will increase in these countries eventually, but this is a paradox with an aging population, as empirical evidence suggests that an aging society tends to save less.

An addition to the burden is that pension reserves that had been built up during the past decade have been affected heavily due to the stock market correction of 2007–2008, which wiped out the previous gains. The IMF estimated that losses in the United States and United Kingdom during 2008 were, respectively, 22 and 31 percent of GDP. These are considerable losses. Pension entitlements are also unlikely to be met without considerable stress. Across the pension industry in Europe and the United States, overambitious payout schemes have been promised to future retirees. An industry standard practice is to commit to 6 percent compounding returns until retirement age. These returns were plausible during the 1980s and 1990s; however the low-yield environment in place since 2001 has changed the investment climate drastically.

The law of compounding interests can quickly turn against a fund manager that is required to return 6 percent year after year. In this example an annual loss of 30 percent makes it almost impossible to meet stated promises in 20 years' time, unless much higher risks are taken in the interim.

The United States faces this problem in its private pension schemes. However, the mismatches between its long-dated pension liabilities and its reserves are jeopardizing the country's public finances still further. According to a report by the Pew Center (a U.S. think tank), the 50 states on aggregate have accumulated more than $3.3 trillion in long-term liabilities (between 2008 and 2030) in pensions, health care, and other benefits that are committed to their employees and those who have already retired. However, the states have made a provision of only $1 trillion of reserves against this liability. Since U.S. states are legally obliged to have a balanced budget at the end of each fiscal year, there are logically only two outcomes: Either they will eventually default under these liabilities, with disastrous consequences for retirees, or the federal government will have to bail them out, adding still further to the U.S. deficit.

A NEW ECONOMIC ENVIRONMENT

The impact of high government debts on future economic growth must be borne in mind. Reinhart and Rogoff (2008), in their study of the interconnection between these two parameters conclude that real GDP, adjusted after inflation, falls by 1 percent when a country's debt-to-GDP ratio rises above 90 percent of GDP. When external debt (taking into account private and corporate debt) rises above 60 percent of GDP, this will deduct another 2 percent of GDP growth, and in case of higher levels, growth could even drop by 50 percent.[8]

This scenario is in line with the findings of the McKinsey study illustrated in Figure 7.1, and can also be compared to the *new normal*, the term used by Mohamed El-Erian, the chief investment officer of PIMCO, to describe the future economic environment. El-Erian has stated:

> *Global growth will be subdued for a while and unemployment high; a heavy hand of government will be evident in several sectors; the core of the global system will be less cohesive and, with the magnet of the Anglo-Saxon model in retreat, finance will no longer be accorded a preeminent role in post-industrial economies. Moreover, the balance of risk will tilt over time toward higher sovereign risk, growing inflationary expectations and stagflation.*[9]

The high inflation environment that has been empirically identified by Reinhart and Rogoff is often accompanied by a currency crisis. Devaluations were common practice during the 1980s among Western European countries that were burdened by high debt. In addition to Belgium and Italy, mentioned earlier, France, Ireland, Denmark, and Sweden used devaluation as a means by which outstanding debts could be brought under control.

In general, a government can devalue its currency in order to erode the value of its debt. A devaluation is in effect almost a default on government debt. However, a devaluation is not a free lunch: It carries risks as well as benefits. Following a devaluation, a country will find it more difficult to obtain future funding from foreign countries, which was, for example, what happened to Russia in the late 1990s and Argentina in 2001. In addition, interest rates often start rising rapidly, to combat the rise in inflation. The end result is a rising spiral of interest rate hikes in the attempt to get inflation back under control. This in turn will affect consumer confidence and have a negative effect on economic growth.

A similar sort of scenario is now in place following the crisis of 2007–2009. Although by no means an official devaluation, pound sterling (GBP) lost 30 percent of its value from August 2007 to December 2009. Together with the United States, the UK banking industry was hard hit among the G7 countries, and due to its economic dependence on banking (above 20 percent of GDP) its economy suffered a proportionate impact. Not being a member of the eurozone gave the United Kingdom the advantage of a kind of devaluation, as the currency dropped in value and thus generated some competitive edge over its trade partners.

Southern eurozone members have begun experiencing sovereign debt pressure on the international capital markets since the end of 2009, with Greece suffering particularly. Its bond yields reached over 300 basis points (bps) above equivalent-tenor German bond yields in February 2010, up from less than 100 bps in 2007. The risk of contagion in other southern eurozone countries is high, which may also threaten the euro project in the long term. Professor Milton Friedman had warned about the survivability of the euro a year before he died:

> *The euro is going to be a big source of problems, not a source of help. The euro has no precedent. To the best of my knowledge, there has never been a monetary union, putting out a fiat currency, composed of independent states. There have been unions based on gold or silver, but not on fiat money—money tempted to inflate—put out by politically independent entities.*[10]

At the time of this writing, there were signs of divergence between core euro members such as Germany, the Netherlands, and France on the one hand and southern European countries such as Portugal, Italy, Greece, and Spain on the other.

A similar sort of problem confronts the United States, which has significant amounts of its debt held by China, Japan, and Russia. China and Russia appeared concerned that the United States might consider using the devaluation tool. This was evident from the tensions at the G20 summit in London in April 2009. At this event the so-called BRIC countries (Brazil, Russia, India, and China) had called for a new international currency to replace the U.S. dollar. Of course, such a replacement currency is many years away.

The United States has a potentially vulnerable exposure in its dependency on funding from foreign countries. This was apparent from the comments by Henry Paulson, former secretary of state under the Bush administration, who stated that a senior Russian politician had negotiated with Chinese government officials about jointly selling holdings of Fannie Mae and Freddie Mac bonds. Although China rejected the proposal, nevertheless this shows the delicate position the United States is in with regard to the financing of its deficit.[11]

THE INFLATION DRAGON

The environment described thus far will have a significant influence on the investment environment. For investors it is vital to take into account the impact of the macroeconomic situation, particularly with regard to sovereign debt, and its effect on asset classes. This is a challenging exercise, but we use it as the background in formulating the new investment model.

Our first focus is on inflation and the damage it can do to investment policy and savings. Based on the debate we reviewed earlier in this chapter, there is a significant probability that inflation will return to be a problem in the second half of this decade, and beyond. As Figure 7.1 suggests, there will not be an immediate pickup in inflation, because of the amount of deleveraging that the global economy still needs to work through. The process of deleveraging will keep inflation at bay, but after 2015 this situation may well reverse.

Inflation remains on the agenda because of the extent of the various stimulus packages that governments and central banks deployed to counter the effects of the financial crash of 2007–2009. These measures cannot be removed immediately; rather, they will be wound down gradually over time, thereby keeping alive a risk of inflationary pressures arising in due course. With regard to monetary policy, there is a real risk that the U.S. Federal Reserve, the Bank of England, and to a lesser extent the European Central Bank (ECB) run the risk of mistiming their policy response. Another factor driving increased inflation risk is the aging population we described earlier. In a scenario where governments do not take the drastic policy measures that are necessary to cope with the issue of demographic change, inflation will be a high risk factor.

The impact of inflation is felt over a prolonged period of time. Inflation erodes capital on a daily basis in only a minor way; however, over time the erosion of an investment is significant because of the compounding effect. We can illustrate this with a simple arithmetic example. At an inflation rate of 3.5 percent, which does not look very high, €2,500 a month spent today will buy only €1,256 worth of goods and services 20 years from now. This is a loss of 50 percent of one's living standard if not corrected for inflation.

In Table 7.5 we illustrate the impact of different inflation rates on buying power. Together with the loss of buying power, the value of wealth will erode over time. At an inflation rate of 3.5 percent, €100,000 today will be worth only €50,257 in 20 years, which is again a loss in value of 50 percent.

Thus inflation remains an important factor when setting return on investment requirements now, compared to the previous decade when inflation was low (see Figure 7.4).

The Inflation Solution

Given, therefore, that the Western world is faced with an inflationary environment over the next 5 to 15 years, the first guideline for an investment

TABLE 7.5   Impact of Inflation on Consumption Budget

Value of EUR 2,500 at Various Inflation Rates

Inflation Rate	Amount to Spend over 20 Years	Reduction in Living Standard
2	EUR 1,682	33%
3	EUR 1,384	45%
4	EUR 1,141	54%
5	EUR 942	62%
6	EUR 780	69%
7	EUR 646	74%
8	EUR 536	79%

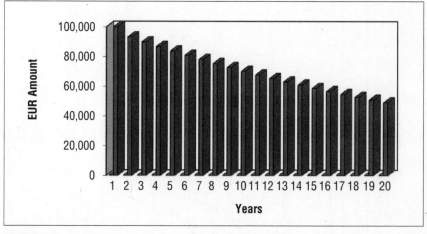

FIGURE 7.4   Impact of Inflation on Wealth

portfolio manager is to build an element of inflation protection into the portfolio. There are a number of possibilities or instruments available with which to undertake this.

The most obvious choice is the government index-linked bond market. The U.S. Treasury issues inflation-indexed Treasuries, or TIPS, on a regular basis. Redemption of capital is linked to the U.S. Consumer Price Index (CPI), which reflects U.S. inflation. With such an instrument the investor is protected against inflation. TIPS are available in maturities of 5-year, 10-year, and 20-year.

An overview of inflation-linked bonds issued by selected governments around the world is shown in Table 7.6.

TABLE 7.6 Inflation-Linked Bonds Issued by Selected Governments

Country	Issue	Issuer	Inflation Index
United States	Treasury Inflation-Protected Securities (TIPS)	U.S. Treasury	U.S. Consumer Price Index
United States	Series I Inflation-Indexed Savings Bonds (I-Bonds)	U.S. Treasury	U.S. Consumer Price Index
United Kingdom	Inflation-Linked Gilt (ILG)	UK Debt Management Office	Retail Price Index (RPI)
France	OAT and OATi	Agence France Trésor	France CPI ex-tobacco (OATi), EU HICP* (OAT€i)
Canada	Real Return Bond (RRB)	Bank of Canada	Canada All-Items CPI
Australia	Capital Indexed Bonds (CAIN series)	Department of the Treasury (Australia)	Weighted average of eight capital cities: All-Groups Index
Germany	Bund index and BO index	Bundesrepublik Deutschland Finanzagentur	EU HICP* ex-tobacco
Greece	GGBei	Central Bank of Greece	EU HICP ex-tobacco
Italy	BTP€i	Department of the Treasury	EU HICP* ex-tobacco
Japan	JGBi	Ministry of Finance (Japan)	Japan CPI (nationwide, ex-fresh-food)
Sweden	Index-linked Treasury bonds	Swedish National Debt Office	Swedish CPI

*Harmonised Index of Consumer Prices.
Source: Choudhry (2005).

In addition to government-issue inflation bonds, there are also medium-term notes linked to a specific index that are structured by banks. For an investor, the key is to choose a bank seller that has a reasonably high credit rating, because with these notes one has credit exposure on the issuer.

During the past decade, an era of low inflation and interest rates, structured products that were inflation-linked fell in popularity; however, in the wake of the crash they have become more noticeable. Banks have addressed this concern among investors and developed solutions to cover this risk. There is a growing demand from institutional and private investors that wish to safeguard their capital against inflation erosion. Private investors typically desire an end return that is the same effective original amount at the time of their retirement age.

Consider the following scenario: A high-net-worth individual (HNWI) has built up a cash reserve of €5 million, excluding his property, during his career. He and his wife would like to retire but their main worry is whether they can afford to maintain their current living standard. Their preference is to remain for the next 10 years in their current residence, and their children are yet to finish the university. Bearing this in mind, they need to draw €150,000 every year from their capital to cover these costs and to fulfill their retirement plans.

Assuming that they choose an investment product that captures the next 10 years, the solution might look as follows:

Bank-Issued Inflation-Linked Note

Maturity	10 years
Amount	EUR 5 mm
Annual Coupon	EUR 150,000 × Inflation index at year n/Inflation index at starting year
Redemption	EUR 5 mm × Inflation index at ending year/Inflation index at starting year

The note should guarantee that the couple's living standard will keep track with inflation year on year. In addition to this, their capital is redeemed at 100 percent in real terms, and not nominal terms.

This example is tailor-made for an investor who still needs an intermediate income from his investments. Other solutions are available that would be suitable for pension funds. In this case the structure would build in a compounded coupon, which was paid out at maturity together with the inflation-adjusted capital.

Under the assumption that inflation is at 3.00 percent annually (year-on-year) and a compounded coupon of 2.80 percent would be paid out after 10 years, the investment would look as follows:

Maturity	n years
Amount	EUR 10 mm
Compounded Coupon	Capital $\times [1 + \text{coupon}]^n - 1]$
Redemption	$\text{Capital} \times \left[\dfrac{\text{inflationindex}_{end}}{\text{inflationindex}_{start}} - 1 \right]$

Table 7.7 illustrates the investment's payoff schedule.

The advantage of this structure is that it benefits from the compounding effect of the incorporated coupon. In order to achieve 100 percent protection against inflation, one needs a funding level above Euribor or LIBOR. One has to take into account that the higher the compounded coupon an investor aims for, the higher the funding level needs to be, and as a result the higher the credit risk is. In addition to the level of inflation, there are two other parameters that influence this spread level: the type of inflation index chosen and the level of long-term interest rates.

Equity Versus Credit

There is an ongoing discussion on whether equities present good protection against inflation risks. There are strong reasons with which one can counter this argument. First, in a rising-inflation environment, interest rates would also rise, and this factor is negatively correlated with equity markets. We must also consider whether companies are free to raise the prices of goods and services to keep pace with inflation, a common assumption in equity investment analysis. However, this is a misconception. Corporate profits

TABLE 7.7 Investment Payoff Schedule

	HICP	Inflation	Cumulated Coupon	Invested Capital	Total Maturity
Start	108.63		2.80%	10,000,000.00	
Year 1	111.89	3.00%	—	—	
Year 2	115.25	3.00%	—	—	
Year 3	118.70	3.00%	—	—	
Year 4	122.26	3.00%	—	—	
Year 5	125.93	3.00%	—	—	
Year 6	129.71	3.00%	—	—	
Year 7	133.60	3.00%	—	—	
Year 8	137.61	3.00%	—	—	
Year 9	141.74	3.00%	—	—	
Year 10	145.99	3.00%	3,180,477.58	13,439,163.79	16,619,641.37

are the result of the difference between the cost of commodities and the cost of finished goods. Since inflation typically finds its origin in the commodity sector, corporations cannot increase their prices until margins are squeezed down. Therefore, it is actually quite difficult to maintain profitability in an inflationary environment.

A more important reason why one should not view equities as an alternative investment product to counter inflation is the volatility factor. Typically in a wealth management case, the investor is looking for a stable income and capital preservation. Equities cannot offer this because of their higher price volatility compared to bonds, and the uncertainty that surrounds most companies' dividend policies.

Further, there is the risk profile of equities compared to bonds. In the event of default of an underlying issuer, bonds still offer an element of recovery value. Equities do not. This is because bondholders are more senior in the debt capital structure than shareholders, who are at the bottom of the creditor hierarchy. This issue was apparent after the bankruptcy of Lehman Brothers.

There are several examples from the past that show the different end results of these two asset classes after the occurrence of a bankruptcy or credit event. Figures 7.5 and 7.6 show the difference between the bond and

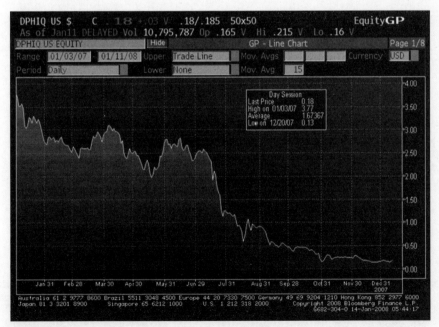

FIGURE 7.5 Fall in Delphi Stock Price in Period Leading Up to Bankruptcy
Source: © Bloomberg Finance L.P. All rights reserved. Used with permission.

	Recovery Rate (%)
Bank Debt	77.5
Senior Secured Bonds	62.0
Senior Unsecured Bonds	42.6
Senior Subordinated Bonds	30.3
Subordinated Bonds	292
Junior Subordinated Bonds	19.1

Note: Recoveries are discounted at each instrument's pre-default interest rate

FIGURE 7.6 Recovery Rates on Delphi Debt Following Bankruptcy
Source: Standard & Poor's Risk Solutions LossStats Database.

the stock of Delphi at the time of its bankruptcy in 2005. Figure 7.5 shows the fall in the equity price; however, we see from Figure 7.6 that the senior unsecured bond of Delphi still had a recovery value of above 40 percent. However the equity was left essentially worthless.

The bankruptcy of Japan Airlines in 2010 again illustrates this phenomenon. In this case the recovery value of the bonds was relatively low compared to recent historical comparisons. Nevertheless, Figure 7.7 shows how the stock fell in value compared to a recovery value of (on average) 25 percent of the outstanding bonds.

To the main methods of protecting an investment against inflation erosion, via government bonds or structured notes issued by banks, we may add a third technique. This is via exchange-traded funds (ETFs). We review this product later in the chapter.

Sovereign Bonds

The second topic for consideration in the asset allocation decision is sovereign bonds. Earlier in this chapter we discussed some of the risks involved with government risk. Based on recent research such as that

FIGURE 7.7 Japan Airlines Stock Price History, 2009–2010
Source: © Bloomberg Finance L.P. All rights reserved. Used with permission.

from Reinhart and Rogoff (2007) and what we concluded from developments in 2010 in the southern eurozone, it can be seen that it is necessary to build protection against this risk into an investment portfolio. We described the issues around countries such as the United States, the United Kingdom, Japan, and eurozone members and the aging of their populations. Thus there is an increased risk that in this environment credit spreads on government bonds will rise considerably during the next decade.

In 2005 Standard & Poor's simulated the rating evolution of the United Kingdom, the United States, France, and Germany. In this pre-crisis period, all countries were expected to lose their AAA rating between 2015 and 2025, down to BBB– by 2035 at the latest. In the meantime, conditions deteriorated.[12] This is not a matter of predicting whether one of these countries will default under its debt. However, we do anticipate increased volatility on certain sovereign names. In some cases it is impossible to avoid investing in sovereign credit. Pension funds, insurance companies, and banks are often obliged to invest in government bonds.

In such cases, therefore, it is important to build protection into their portfolios. This can be done by buying protection on the respective sovereign name using credit default swaps. This would not be a perfect hedge, but overlapping a period of five years of credit exposure will certainly give a more comfortable buffer against potential turmoil.

Institutional investors such as pension funds and insurance companies have long-dated government bonds on their books with maturities of 20 to 30 years and even longer. So building in protection for the next, say, five years would at least offer a level of protection. It provides the investor a certain amount of time in which to observe how the sovereign debt issues are performing, and how they are likely to perform over the next half decade.

This is not the perfect solution as in some cases it may already be too late to buy protection, due to the expense associated with it. For example, in February 2010, Greek sovereign credit default swap (CDS) price levels reached 500 bps. However, there are a number of sovereign names where the market is underestimating or underpricing the risk for the time being. This list might include countries such as the United States, the United Kingdom, Japan, France, and Belgium.

The worst-case scenario if this view is wrong is that it will reduce the portfolio yield by the cost of protection. However, if the market suffers any debt worries or volatility, this type of insurance will be invaluable and will also return a mark-to-market yield enhancement. Investors may consider this as analogous to fire insurance on a house.

We do realize that buying this credit protection can contribute to further systemic risk. If the majority of the institutional investment community all came to a similar conclusion, and placed credit protection on major sovereign names, the risk would end up being housed within a relatively small number of counterparties. We observed in Chapter 2 on systemic risk that this is already an issue in the derivatives market, where a small number of U.S. investment banks carry the ultimate risk exposure. If there ever was a credit event on one of these sovereign names, these banks would be liable for billions if not trillions of dollars in credit payments to their counterparties.

Investors who have the choice and flexibility to avoid sovereign names should keep this in mind as there is also some currency risk linked to these countries. Countries such as Germany, the Netherlands, Norway, and Canada may provide safe-haven investment exits, although the last two still present currency risk for non-eurozone-based investors.

This brings us to the next asset class that needs to be handled with care in the investment portfolio, that of currencies.

CURRENCIES AND A CHANGING GEOPOLITICAL LANDSCAPE

We agree with the conclusion by Reinhart and Rogoff that currency crises are inherent with sovereign crises. Four currency blocks will generate increased risk: the British pound (GBP), the U.S. dollar (USD), the euro (EUR), and the Japanese yen (JPY).

Devaluation is a useful tool for governments looking to reduce the value of their debt. This is certainly valid where the outstanding debt is in part financed by foreigners, as is the case for the United States. Russia's strong economic recovery during the past decade was also due to the merits of the devaluation of the Russian ruble. Of course it is not a painless option for governments, as the outcome is that it makes it more difficult to raise loans from foreign investors in the future. Devaluation reduces the pressure on a government in debt, but it does not provide new future funding.

Large foreign-exchange reserve holders such as the GCC countries, the BRIC countries, and Russia appear to be increasingly worried about the potential danger that the United States will allow its currency to devalue further. During the G20 summit in April 2009 there were some nonstarter diplomatic conversations behind the scenes, looking at the possibility of replacing the USD as the world's reserve currency. While this is a live issue, for a workable alternative to the U.S. dollar to arise, and one that replicated its liquidity, it would require some considerable effort and unity of action, as well as some considerable time. It is something that is some years away from being a possibility. Investors will have to live with the issues that arise from the world's use of the dollar as a reserve currency for some time yet.

The reemergence of Russia and the BRICs in general shows that there are new dynamics at play in the global economy that will have an impact on investor asset allocation. The developed markets are, following the crisis, driven by government support and stock rebuilding. This is in line with Minsky's "big government" thesis for the circumstances in place during the aftermath of a credit crisis.[13]

Emerging markets (EMs) were the driving global economic growth engine in the aftermath of the crash of 2007–2009. They will play a pivotal role in the new investment paradigm as well. India and Brazil are high on the future investor's list, and rank above Russia and China, two countries that still lack legal transparency and political stability.

The emerging Indian economy is expected to be a major target for foreign investors' funds. More importantly, it has a stable political climate and a highly educated labor force. In the next decade India will present serious competitive pressures to the Western service industry. One example will suffice. Thomas Friedman describes the competition that Indian radiologists are creating for U.S. specialized medical personnel. He cites the case of X-rays and scans taken from U.S. patients being e-mailed to India overnight, where a cheaper but equally qualified Indian radiologist can write a report and send it back to the United States for explanation and use in the diagnosis for the patient.[14] The Western publishing industry has also taken advantage of Indian human capital skills to move much of its production process to the subcontinent.

Brazil is attractive for other reasons. Although it has a history of sharp currency fluctuations, which were typically debt-related, the country has experienced a turnaround. Until recently Brazil was confronted with an energy paradox. The country was heavily dependent on energy imports even though the country itself is rich in natural resources. However, as Brazil became more stable it attracted foreign investors and simultaneously it saw, after a heavy devaluation, a correction in its current account and trade balance. For instance, agriculture-related commodities are becoming a valuable asset for the country. The trade balance has turned positive and the country is gradually reducing its outstanding debt.

Investors, therefore, will want to consider these two of the BRIC countries in their asset allocation, given the near certainty that their share of world GDP, both absolute output and growth, will be exponentially higher in 10 years' time than where it is now.

The Commodity Factor

The last asset class we consider is commodities. They are closely related to the emerging market theme we introduced earlier in the discussion on the BRICs. Here it is important to pick out the right type of natural resources to invest in, as they will not rise in value in equal amounts. In general, raw materials that are used in the construction industry will remain in high demand for as long as the expansion process in Asia continues (which we expect will be at least the next decade, if not two). China is playing a dominant role in this, as it continues to build up stocks in different types of natural resources. The government has increased its level of political influence in Africa with this specific purpose in mind.

Taking into account the potential risk of increased inflation and pressures on sovereign debt, gold will continue to play a major role as an asset class. This despite the fact that since the 1980s gold has been a poor hedge against inflation, but its store of value on an emotional level remains undiminished. During periods of perceived U.S. dollar weakness particularly, investors move into gold. This was what was widely believed to be behind

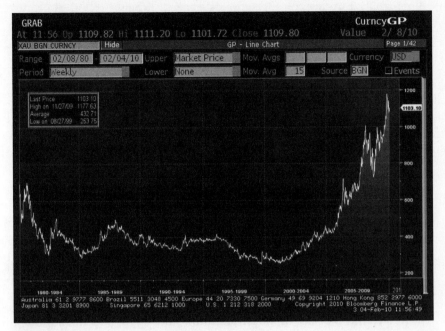

FIGURE 7.8 Evolution of Gold Price since 1980
Source: © Bloomberg Finance L.P. All rights reserved. Used with permission.

central banks such as India, Russia, and China shifting part of their currency reserves into gold during 2009 and 2010.

Gold performs well in times of crisis, and in times of fear of future crises. Figure 7.8 is a chart of the gold price from 1980.

The crisis of 2007–2009 brought this fear back to the front stage. Going forward, at times when major sovereigns are threatened with a loss of their AAA rating this fear will return, and at periods like this gold will outperform. In this respect gold certainly is a good fear hedge.

A specific class of commodities deserves attention: agricultural commodities such as wheat, corn, soybeans, and grains. We expect these to play a major role as a separate asset class in this century. There are a number of reasons for this. First, due to globalization the living standard in emerging markets is rising. Second, also connected with globalization and U.S. cultural hegemony, Westernization of the world is markedly changing food habits around the world. This will result in the demand side for such products rising.

However, it is not clear that the supply side can keep up with this increasing demand, and stocks across the world are not high. The global warming debate contributes to this risk: As governments become ecologically friendlier, for example by promoting biofuels as an alternative to oil and coal, the growth of available supplies is not affected. In the event of, for example, a natural disaster or extreme weather conditions, the supply side will be disrupted. Agricultural commodities, and the companies connected with producing, distributing, and selling them, are expected to gain in value in the next decade.

Among natural resources there is one more specific commodity that is going to play an important role in the next decade: water. We will leave any discussion about global warming to one side. The simple reason for water being a pivotal asset class is the rise of the world's population. Since the 1950s the number of people on our planet has more than doubled. Simultaneously the use of water has tripled. To put this issue in perspective, global population in 1950 was 2,521 billion, compared to 6,707 billion in 2008 (these are UN figures), while with regard to consumption of water, based upon findings published by the UN Food and Agriculture Organization (FAO), the consumption of water has been rising twice as fast as global population grows since the beginning of the twentieth century.

Add to this the pace of industrialization since 1945, and globalization, has impacted the environment and created pollution and environmental damage, which shrinks available water sources. Not all of the water available on the planet can be used for consumption. Only a fraction, approximately 3 percent of it, is ready for use. The vast majority is packed in permanent ice.

This makes water a great investment opportunity for the future. Ideally the investor should invest in pure water as directly as possible, as opposed to picking out a series of venture capital events that work on technological development related to filtration and desalination. The risk here is once again that one needs an element of luck to pick out the winners from the losers. Water itself can be brought down to a pure supply and demand play. Institutional and sophisticated investors have more tools available to play the interest rate/inflation, currency, commodity, and emerging market theme, and can replicate this approach to water as an asset class.

EXCHANGE-TRADED FUNDS: A FLEXIBLE ASSET CLASS

There is an investment tool that in our opinion would be very suitable for smaller investors to play the asset rotation strategy we have discussed in this chapter: exchange-traded funds (ETFs). We define an ETF as a static (mutual) fund, listed as a security on the stock exchange. The ETF can be linked to various asset classes, and gives the investor the opportunity to go long and/or short the underlying asset.

There are several advantages linked to ETF investing. These include:

- *Price and investment transparency.* An ETF is listed as a share on the stock market, so its value trades on a minute-by-minute basis and gives the investor the ability to know the value of his investment at any moment in time. This also means that the holder of an ETF can decide to sell the investment at any time. This contrasts with a mutual fund where one usually has to wait for the closing of the day. Also due to its stock market quotation, the entrance investment amount is lower than for a mutual fund. In many cases it is as low as $100.

  The asset class in which the ETF is invested is determined up front and cannot be changed. It is completely static. Mutual funds, by contrast, continuously change their portfolio, and information is only disclosed on a monthly basis (best case).

- *Cost efficiency.* Compared to mutual funds, ETFs are more cost friendly. There are no hidden management fees or performance fees. Neither are there exit fees should one want to sell the investment. Again, this contrasts with mutual funds, which often work to discourage entry into and exit out of the fund. This also offers the advantage that the ETF investor can work with stop-loss orders without penalty.

- *Long/short capability.* With an ETF an investor has the possibility to go either long or short the market. It is, of course, important to pick out the correct ETF. Being able to short the market offers the investor the ability to use the ETF either as a directional play or as a hedging tool against a portfolio.

  Because investing in an ETF is similar to buying a share, this avoids the problem of margin calls which often are related to shorting. For example, if one buys a future or sells an option, one needs to monitor this position on a daily basis, and margin calls can emerge. With an ETF, the investor knows from the beginning what the total exposure and maximum potential loss will be.

- *Leverage.* Again, the investor needs to exercise caution with this, but many ETFs are offered in a leveraged version up to twice and three times the underlying exposure. This can be an advantage to the private investor.

As there are advantages linked to this product, so are there disadvantages linked to an ETF which investors must be aware of. These include:

- *Imperfect tracking.* Although an ETF should follow the underlying asset as its mirror image, it is possible that the ETF does not track the asset on a lockstep basis. Furthermore, if it is a leveraged ETF, the difference can be even greater because the discrepancies start to accumulate.

   This issue certainly exists with commodity-linked ETFs where the fund is using futures to track the underlying commodity. Here the discrepancies arise every time one needs to roll over the future or swap at maturity. This is based upon the *contango* effect, where the future curve for commodities shows an upward sloping curve. The reason behind this is that prices for future delivery of commodities are usually higher, due to storage costs, compared with immediate delivery.

- *Leveraged ETF.* Again, because of the leverage effect behind it, if one's view is wrong, the investment is going to lose value twice or even three times as fast compared to a nonleveraged ETF.

ETF Examples

Because there is a wide range of possibilities to link ETFs to, it is an appropriate instrument to use when considering the asset allocation issues we have discussed in this chapter. For example, with the inflation theme one can use inflation-linked ETFs, which track the performance of government index-linked bonds. A number of the large bulge-bracket investment banks offer such a product, in which the government inflation-protected bond ETF performance corresponds with the price and yield of a government index, comprising selected sovereign-name inflation-linked bonds.

In the case of sovereign debt issues there are a number of ETFs available. For example, Barclays Bank offers the SPDR Barclays Capital International Treasury Bond, which tracks the price and yield of the Barclays Capital Global Treasury ex-U.S. Capped Index. This index consists of government bonds outside the United States, of which Japanese, German, Italian, Belgian, Spanish, Greek, French, Canadian, and Dutch government bonds are the most important.

As far as currencies are concerned, one has a choice between trackers linked to every major G10 currency pair and even emerging market currencies, and between leveraged and nonleveraged product. An example here is the PowerShares DB U.S. Dollar Index Bullish Fund, which tracks the long performance of the USD against a basket of JPY, EUR, GBP, Canadian dollar (CAD), Swedish krona (SEK), and Swiss franc (CHF).

A similar choice is available for a wide range of commodities from precious metals to agricultural resources to gas, oil, biofuels, and water. An example of a commodity-linked ETF is the ETFS Physical Gold fund tracking the price of gold. We note here that the ETF is backed by physically allocated metal bullion which has no credit risk. The security only holds London Bullion Market (LMBA) Good Delivery bars.

In other words, for private investors the ETF offers the possibility of exposure to all the asset classes we have discussed in this chapter.

CONCLUSION

The financial crisis of 2007–2009 will have a major impact on investor thinking and behavior. The government rescue of the banks has further deteriorated already worsening public finances, and this, together with the aging of society, will influence the performance of certain major asset classes.

The amount of outstanding public debt will have an impact on sovereign fixed-income investments. Certain countries face a severe challenge in keeping their funding levels under control, and this will have a negative impact on the performance of their outstanding government bonds. Substantial public deficits and demographic forces will increase inflation risks. As far as the aging of society is concerned, inflation risk will remain due to a combination of a tighter labor market and wage pressures.

In an inflationary environment commodities typically perform well, and due to the changing geopolitical landscape in which the BRIC countries will play a larger role in the global economy, natural resources will become an important asset class to consider as well. The rise of the global population will put further pressure on the availability of certain agricultural products, which will create further inflationary issues.

These factors all drive our model investment portfolio. Actual percentage breakdowns and share of the total portfolio are, of course, a matter for individual investor preference, circumstances, and risk/reward profile. Nevertheless, certain asset classes should be common to everyone's portfolio, and we have discussed these as follows:

- Government bonds.
- Inflation-linked structures.
- Commodities.
- Emerging markets/BRIC country-linked assets.
- Currencies.
- ETFs.

Regarding government bonds, we have shown that the focus should be on those countries with healthy public finances, including those outside the traditional economic Western area such as Singapore.

A protection against inflation can be set up in more than one way. Inflation-linked government bonds are the most obvious solution and are readily available. Of course the choice of a particular country also reflects the extent to which an investor is comfortable with the sovereign issuer. There are also structures available that have been developed by the large banks. Once again the key is to choose a respectable issuer from a credit point of view. Another investment alternative would be to set up protection using ETFs.

The higher growth prospects from the EM countries and the BRICs make these countries an attractive investment target. Again, this can be played in more than one way. Investment can be via the bond market, currency market, ETFs, and of course (for those who still have a preference for equities) via the stock market. We reiterate our preference for bonds over equities due to their senior treatment in the event of issuer defaults.

Playing the government bond market or EMs will automatically generate currency exposure. Currencies will also be an important asset class to consider because of the fact that yield differentials are automatically reflected in currency pairs. As we expect more asset rotation and an ongoing search for safe yields, this will also create currency opportunities but at the same time increase volatility.

In this respect ETFs are once again a solution. Via ETFs the investor can put in place currency trades in a straightforward manner. At the same time, these can be used as a hedging tool against unwanted currency risk.

Our final observation is that capital preservation should always be the key objective in all investment decisions. This is not an issue restricted to those approaching retirement age or the already retired. It is a vital consideration for all investors with a maturity horizon longer than one year. Such an objective will not be achieved via a buy-and-hold strategy, but rather through a long-term outlook and active asset rotation.

CHAPTER 8

Bank Asset-Liability and Liquidity Risk Management

The Western world's banking system was, in some jurisdictions at least, on the brink of collapse in September and October 2008, in the wake of the Lehman bankruptcy. Intervention by governments, which in some cases extended to a blanket guarantee of banks' total liabilities, prevented this collapse from taking place. In the aftermath of the crisis, national regulators and the Bank for International Settlements (BIS) circulated consultative papers and recommendations that addressed new requirements on bank capital, liquidity, and risk management. The United Kingdom's Financial Services Authority (FSA) was perhaps most demanding; in its Policy Statement 09/16, which was issued in October 2009, it outlined measures on capital treatment, liquidity requirements, and stress testing that implied a fundamental change in the bank's business model going forward.

In this and the next chapter, we discuss the implications for banks of the new emphasis on risk management of the regulators and the BIS committee; the latter will issue Basel III rules for implementation from the end of 2012 (although it is likely that practical implementation will be some years after this). We also provide our recommendations on how banks can go about meeting these requirements in a way that generates sustained return on capital. This chapter looks at the fundamentals of asset-liability and liquidity risk management, and how its basic principles need to change in the light of new regulations. In Chapter 9, we consider the implications of these required changes for the basic banking model.

BASIC CONCEPTS OF BANK ASSET-LIABILITY MANAGEMENT

Asset-liability management (ALM) is a generic term that is used to refer to a number of things by different market participants. We define it here as the high-level management of a bank's assets and liabilities; as such it is a strategy-level discipline and not a tactical one. It may be set within a bank's treasury division or by its asset-liability committee (ALCO). The principal objective of the ALM function is to manage interest-rate risk and liquidity risk. It will also set overall policy for credit risk and credit risk management, although tactical-level credit policy is set at a lower level within credit committees. Although the basic tenets of ALM would seem to apply more to commercial banking rather than investment banking, in reality it is important that it is applied to both functions. A trading desk still deals in assets and liabilities, and these must be managed for interest-rate risk and liquidity risk. In a properly integrated banking function the ALM desk will have a remit covering all aspects of a bank's operations.

In financial markets the two main strands of risk management are interest-rate risk and liquidity risk. ALM practice is concerned with managing this risk. Interest-rate risk exists in two strands. The first strand is the more obvious one, the risk of changes in asset and liability values due to changes in interest rates. Such a change impacts the cash flows of assets and liabilities, or their present value, because financial instruments are valued with reference to market interest rates. The second strand is that associated with optionality, which arises with products such as early-redeemable loans. The other main type of risk that ALM seeks to manage is liquidity risk, which refers to both the liquidity of markets and the ease with which assets can be translated into cash.

ALM is conducted primarily at an overview, balance-sheet level. The risk that is managed is an aggregate, group-level risk. This makes sense because one could not manage a viable banking business by leaving interest-rate and liquidity risk management at individual operating levels. Figure 8.1 illustrates the cornerstones of ALM. Essentially, interest-rate risk exposure is managed at the group level by the treasury desk. The drivers are the different currency interest rates, with each exposure being made up of the net present value (NPV) of cash flow as it changes with changes in interest rates. The discount rate used to calculate the NPV is the prevailing market rate for each time bucket in the term structure.

The interest-rate exposure arises because rates fluctuate from day to day, and continuously over time. The primary risk is that of interest-rate reset, for floating-rate assets and liabilities. The secondary risk is liquidity risk: Unless assets and liabilities are matched by amount and term, assets must be funded on a continuous rolling basis. Equally, the receipt of funds must be placed on a continuous basis. Whether an asset carries a fixed- or floating-rate reset will determine its exposure to interest-rate fluctuations. Where an asset is marked at a fixed rate, a rise in rates will reduce its NPV and so reduce its value to the bank. This is intuitively easy to grasp,

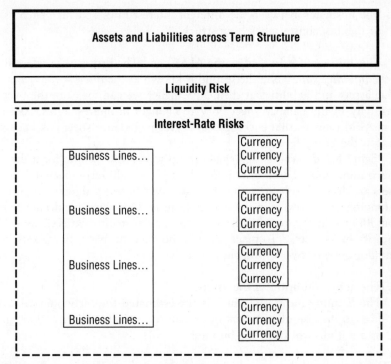

FIGURE 8.1 Cornerstone of ALM Philosophy

even without recourse to financial arithmetic, because we can see that the asset is now paying a below-market rate of interest. Or we can think of it as a loss due to opportunity cost forgone, since the assets are earning below what they could earn if they were employed elsewhere in the market. The opposite applies if there is a fall in rates: This causes the NPV of the asset to rise. For assets marked at a floating rate of interest, the exposure to fluctuating rates is much less, because the rate receivable on the asset will reset at periodic intervals, which will allow for changes in market rates.

We speak of risk exposure as being for the group as a whole. This exposure must therefore aggregate the net risk of all of the bank's operating business. Even for the simplest banking operation, we can see that this will produce a net mismatch between assets and liabilities, because different business lines will have differing objectives for their individual books. This mismatch will manifest itself in two ways:

1. The mismatch between the different terms of assets and liabilities across the term structure.

2. The mismatch between the different interest rates at which each asset or liability contract has been struck.

This mismatch is known as the ALM *gap*.[1] The first type is referred to as the *liquidity gap*, while the second is known as the *interest-rate gap*. We value assets and liabilities at their NPV, hence we can measure the overall sensitivity of the balance sheet NPV to changes in interest rates. As such then, ALM is an art that encompasses aggregate balance-sheet risk management at the group level.

Figure 8.2 shows the aggregate group level ALM profile for a derivatives trading house based in London. There is a slight term mismatch as no assets are deemed to have overnight maturity, whereas a significant portion of funding (liabilities) is in the overnight term. One thing we do not know from looking at Figure 8.2 is how this particular institution is defining the maturity of its assets.[2] To place these in the relevant maturity buckets, one can adopt one of two approaches, namely:

1. The actual duration of the assets.
2. The *liquidity duration*, which is the estimated time it would take the firm to dispose of its assets in an enforced or fire-sale situation, such as a withdrawal from the business.

Each approach has its adherents, and we believe that actually there is no right way. It is up to the individual institution to adopt one method and then consistently adhere to it. The second approach has the disadvantage, however, of being inherently subjective—the estimate of the time taken to dispose of an asset book is not an exact science and is little more than educated guesswork. Nevertheless, for long-dated and/or illiquid assets, it

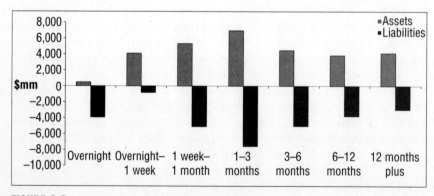

FIGURE 8.2   Derivatives Trading House ALM Profile

is at least a workable method that enables practitioners to work around a specified ALM framework with regard to structuring the liability profile.

Liquidity Gap

There is an obvious risk exposure arising because of liquidity mismatch of assets and liabilities. The maturity terms will not match, which creates the liquidity gap. The amount of assets and liabilities maturing at any one time will also not match (although overall, by definition, assets must equal liabilities). *Liquidity risk* is the risk that a bank will not be able to refinance assets as liabilities become due, for any reason.[3] To manage this risk, the bank will hold a large portion of assets in very liquid form.[4] A surplus of assets over liabilities creates a funding requirement. If there is a surplus of liabilities, the bank will need to find efficient uses for those funds. In either case, the bank has a liquidity gap. This liquidity can be projected over time, so that one knows what the situation is each morning, based on net expiring assets and liabilities. The projection will change daily, of course, due to new business undertaken each day.

We could eliminate liquidity gap risk by matching assets and liabilities across each time bucket. Actually, at the individual loan level this is a popular strategy: If we can invest in an asset paying 5.50 percent for three months and fund this with a three-month loan costing 5.00 percent, we have locked in a 50 basis point gain that is interest-rate risk-free. However, while such an approach can be undertaken at an individual asset level, it would not be possible at an aggregate level, or at least not possible without imposing severe restrictions on the business. Hence, liquidity risk is a key consideration in ALM. A bank with a surplus of long-term assets over short-term liabilities will have an ongoing requirement to fund the assets continuously, and there is the ever-present risk that funds may not be available as and when they are required. The concept of a future funding requirement is itself a driver of interest-rate risk, because the bank will not know what the future interest rates at which it will deal will be.[5] So a key part of ALM involves managing and hedging this forward liquidity risk.

Definition and Illustration   To reiterate, then, the liquidity gap is the difference in maturity between assets and liabilities at each point along the term structure. Because for many banks ALM concerns itself with a medium-term management of risk, this will not be beyond a five-year horizon, and in many cases will be considerably less than this. Note from Figure 8.2 how the longest-dated time bucket in the ALM profile extends out to only "12 months plus," so that all liabilities longer than one year were grouped in one time bucket. This action recognizes that most liabilities are funded in the money markets, although a material proportion of funding should be much longer term, and up to the maximum tenor that the bank is able to obtain.

For each point along the term structure at which a gap exists, there is (liquidity) gap risk exposure. This is the risk that funds cannot be raised as required, or that the rate payable on these funds is prohibitive.[6] To manage this risk, a bank must perforce:

- Disperse the funding profile (the liability profile) over more than just a short period of time. For example, it would be excessively risky to concentrate funding in just the overnight to one-week time bucket, so a bank will spread the profile across a number of time buckets. Figure 8.3 shows the liability profile for a European multicurrency asset-backed commercial paper program, with liabilities extending from one month to one year.
- Manage expectations such that large-size funding requirements are diarized well in advance, as well as not planned for times of low liquidity such as the Christmas and New Year period.
- Hold a significant proportion of assets in the form of very liquid instruments such as very-short-term cash loans, Treasury bills, and high-quality short-term bank certificates of deposit (CDs).

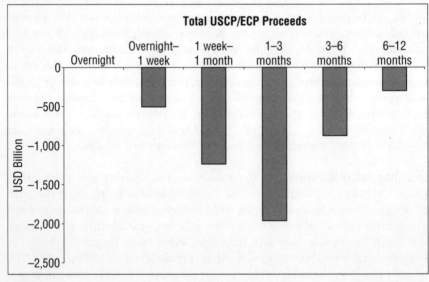

FIGURE 8.3   Commercial Paper Program Liability Profile

The latter means can act as a reserve of liquidity in the event of a funding crisis, because they can be turned into cash at very short notice.

The size of the liquidity gap at any one time is never more than a snapshot in time, because it is constantly changing as new commitments are entered into on both the asset and liability sides. For this reason some writers speak of a *static* gap and a *dynamic* gap, but in practice one recognizes that there is only ever a dynamic gap, because the position changes daily. Hence we will refer only to one liquidity gap.

A further definition is the *marginal* gap, which is the difference between the change in assets and the change in liabilities during a specified time period. This is also known as the *incremental* gap. If the change in assets is greater than the change in liabilities, this is a positive marginal gap, while if the opposite applies it is a negative marginal gap.[7]

We illustrate these values in Figure 8.4. This is a simplified asset-liability profile from a regional European bank, showing gap and marginal gap at each time period. Note that the liabilities have been structured to produce an *ALM smile*, which is recognized to follow prudent business practice. Generally, no more than 20 percent of the total funding should be in the overnight to one-week time bucket, and similarly for the 9- to 12-month bucket. The marginal gap is measured as the difference between the change in assets and the change in liabilities from one period to the next.

Figure 8.4 shows the graphical profile of the numbers in Table 8.1.

Liquidity Risk   Liquidity risk exposure arises from normal banking operations. That is, it exists irrespective of the type of funding gap, be it excess assets over liabilities for any particular time bucket or an excess of liabilities over assets. In other words, there is a funding risk in any case: Either funds must be obtained or surplus assets laid off. The liquidity risk in itself generates interest-rate risk, due to the uncertainty of future interest rates. This risk can be managed through hedging.

TABLE 8.1   Simplified ALM Profile for Regional European Bank

	One Week	One Month	3 Months	6 Months	9–12 Months	>12 Months	Total
Assets	10	90	460	710	520	100	1,890
Liabilities	100	380	690	410	220	90	1,890
Gap	−90	−290	−230	300	300	10	
Marginal gap		200	−60	−530	0	290	

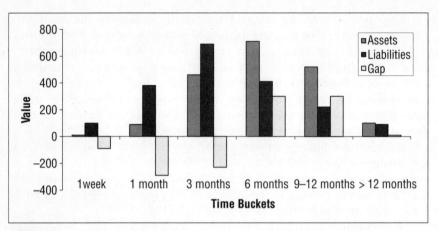

FIGURE 8.4   ALM Time Profile

If assets are floating-rate, there is less concern over interest-rate risk because of the nature of the interest-rate reset. This also applies to floating-rate liabilities, but only insofar as these match floating-rate assets. Floating-rate liabilities issued to fund fixed-rate assets create forward risk exposure to rising interest rates. Note that even if both assets and liabilities are floating-rate, they can still generate interest-rate risk. For example, if assets pay six-month LIBOR and liabilities pay three-month LIBOR, there is an interest-rate spread risk between the two terms. Such an arrangement has eliminated liquidity risk, but not interest-rate spread risk.

Liquidity risk can be managed by matching assets and liabilities, or by setting a series of rolling-term loans to fund a long-dated asset. Generally, however, banks will have a particular view of future market conditions and will manage the ALM book in line with this view. This would leave in place a certain level of liquidity risk.

Matched Book   The simplest way to manage liquidity and interest-rate risk is the *matched book* approach, also known as cash matching. This is actually very rarely observed in practice, even among conservative institutions such as the smaller UK building societies. In matched book, assets and liabilities, and their time profiles, are matched as closely as possible. This includes allowing for the amortization of assets.[8] As well as matching maturities and time profiles, the interest-rate basis for both assets and liabilities will be matched. That is, fixed loans to fund fixed-rate assets, and floating-rate loans for floating-rate assets and liabilities. Floating-rate instruments will further need to match the period of each interest-rate reset, to eliminate spread risk.

Under a matched book or *cash flow matching* approach, in theory there is no liquidity gap. Locking in terms and interest rate bases will also lock in profit. For instance, a six-month fixed-rate loan is funded with a six-month fixed-rate deposit. This would eliminate both liquidity risk and interest-rate risk. In a customer-focused business it will not be possible to precisely match assets and liabilities, but from a macro level it should be possible to match the profiles fairly closely, by netting total exposure on both sides and matching this. Of course, it may not be desirable to run a matched book, as this would mean the ALM book was not taking any view at all on the path of future interest rates. Hence a part of the book is usually left unmatched, and it is this part that will benefit (or lose out) if rates go the way they are expected to (or not!).

Managing the Gap with Undated Assets and Liabilities   We have described a scenario of liquidity management where the maturity date of both assets and liabilities is known with certainty. However, a large part of retail and commercial banking operations revolves around assets that do not have an explicit maturity date. These include current account overdrafts and credit card balances. They also include drawn and undrawn lines of credit. The volume of these assets is a function of general economic conditions and can be difficult to predict. Banks will need to be familiar with their clients' behavior and their requirements over time to be able to assess when and for how long these assets will be utilized.

Undated assets are balanced on the other side by nondated liabilities, such as non-interest-bearing liabilities (NIBLs) which include checking accounts and instant-access deposit accounts. The latter frequently attract very low rates of interest and may be included in the NIBL total. Undated liabilities are treated in different ways by banks; the most common treatment places these funds in the shortest time bucket, the overnight-to-one-week bucket. However, this means the firm's gap and liquidity profile can be highly volatile and unpredictable, which places greater strain on ALM management. For this reason some banks take the opposite approach and place these funds in the longest-dated bucket, the greater-than-12-month bucket. A third approach is to split the total undated liabilities into a *core* balance and an *unstable* balance, and place the first in the longest-dated bucket and the second in the shortest-dated bucket. The amount recognized as the core balance will need to be analyzed over time, to make sure that is accurate.

Managing Liquidity

Managing liquidity gaps and the liquidity process is a continuous, dynamic one because the ALM profile of a bank changes on a daily basis. Liquidity management is the term used to describe this continuous process of raising and laying off funds, depending on whether one is long or short cash that day.

The basic premise is a simple one: The bank must be squared off by the end of each day, which means that the net cash position is zero. Thus liquidity management is both very short-term as well as projected over the long term, because every position put on today creates a funding requirement in the future on its maturity date. The ALM desk must be aware of the future funding or excess cash positions and act accordingly, whether this means raising funds now or hedging forward interest-rate risk.

The Basic Case: The Funding Gap   A funding requirement is dealt with on the day it occurs. The decision on how it will be treated will factor the term that is put on, as well as allowing for any new assets put on that day. As funding is arranged, the gap at that day will be zero. The next day, there will be a new funding requirement, or surplus, depending on the net position of the book.

This is illustrated in Figure 8.5. Starting from a flat position on the first day (t_0) we observe a gap (the dotted line) on t_1, which is closed by putting on funding to match the asset maturity. The amount of funding to raise, and the term to run it to, will take into account the future gap as well as that day's banking activities. So at t_2 we observe a funding excess, which is then laid off. We see at t_3 that the assets invested run beyond the maturity of the liabilities at t_2, so we have a funding requirement again at t_3. The decision on the term and amount will be based on the market view of the ALM desk. A matched-book approach may well be taken if

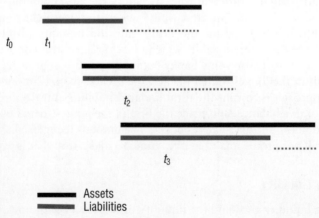

FIGURE 8.5   Funding Position on a Daily Basis

the desk does not have a strong view, or if its view is at odds with market consensus.

There are also external factors to take into account. For instance, the availability of funds in the market may be limited, due to both macro-level issues and the bank's own ability to raise funds. The former might be during times of market correction or recession (a credit crunch), while the latter includes the bank's credit lines with market counterparties. Also, some funds will have been raised in the capital markets and this cash will cover part of the funding requirement. In addition, the ALM desk must consider the cost of the funds it is borrowing; if, for example, it thought that interest rates in the short term, and for short-term periods, were going to fall, it might cover the gap with only short-term funds so it can then refinance at the expected lower rates. The opposite might be done if the desk thought rates would rise in the near future.

Running a liquidity gap over time, beyond customer requirements, would reflect a particular view of the ALM desk. So maintaining a consistently underfunded position suggests that interest rates are expected to decline, at which point longer-term funds can be taken at cost. Maintaining an overfunded gap would imply that the bank thinks rates will be rising, and so longer-term funds are locked in now at lower interest rates. Even if the net position is dictated by customer requirements (for example, customers placing more on deposit than they take out in loans), the bank can still manage the resultant gap in the wholesale market.

Having excess liabilities generally is a rare scenario at a bank and is not, under most circumstances, a desirable position to be in. This is because the bank will have target return-on-capital (ROC) ratios to achieve, and this requires that funds be put to work, so to speak, by acquiring assets. In the case of equity capital it is imperative that these funds are properly employed.[9] The exact structure of the asset book will depend on the bank's view on interest rates and the yield curve generally. The shape of the yield curve and expectations on this will also influence the structure and tenor of the asset book. The common practice is to spread assets across the term structure, with varying maturities. There will also be investments made with a forward start date, to lock in rates in the forward curve now. Equally, some investments will be made for very short periods so that if interest rates rise, when the funds are reinvested they will benefit from the higher rates.

The Liquidity Ratio

The *liquidity ratio* is the ratio of assets to liabilities. It is a short-term ratio, usually calculated for the money market term only—that is, up to one year. Under most circumstances, and certainly under a positive yield curve environment, it would be expected to be above 1. However, this is less common at the very short end because the average tenor of assets is often greater than the average tenor of liabilities. So in the one-month to three-month period, and perhaps out to the six-month, the ratio may well be less than 1. This reflects the fact that short-term borrowing is used to fund longer-term assets.

A ratio of below 1 is inefficient from a return-on-equity (ROE) point of view. It represents an opportunity cost of return forgone. To manage it, banks may invest more funds in the very short term, but this also presents its own problems because the return on these assets may not be sufficient. This is especially true in a positive yield curve environment. This is one scenario where a matched book approach will be prudent, because the bank should be able to lock in a bid-offer spread in the very short end of the yield curve.[10] A more risky approach would be to lend in the short term and fund these in the long term, but this would create problems because the term premium in the yield curve will make borrowing in the long term expensive relative to the return on short-dated assets (unless we have an inverted yield curve). There is also the liquidity risk associated with the more frequent rolling over of assets compared to liabilities. We see, then, that maintaining the liquidity ratio carries something of a cost for banks.

ASSET AND LIABILITY MANAGEMENT: THE ALCO

The ALM reporting process is often overseen by the bank's asset-liability management committee (ALCO). The ALCO will have a specific remit to oversee all aspects of asset-liability management, from the front-office money market function to back-office operations and middle-office reporting and risk management. In this chapter we consider the salient features of ALCO procedures.

ALCO Policy

The ALCO is responsible for setting, and implementing, the ALM policy. Its composition varies in different banks but usually includes heads of business lines as well as director-level staff such as the finance director. The ALCO also sets hedging policy. Typical membership of ALCO is as follows:

Members
CFO (chairman); deputy (head of financial accounting)
CEO (deputy chairman)

Head of treasury; deputy (head of money markets)
Managing director, commercial banking
Managing director, retail banking
Chief risk officer

Guests
Head of market and liquidity risk
Head of product control
Head of ALM/money markets
Head of financial institutions

Secretary
Personal assistant to the head of treasury

The ALM process may be undertaken by the treasury desk, ALM desk, or other dedicated function within the bank. In traditional commercial banks it will be responsible for management reporting to the asset-liability management committee (ALCO). The ALCO will consider the report in detail at regular meetings, usually weekly. Main points of interest in the ALCO report include variations in interest income, the areas that experienced fluctuations in income, and what the latest short-term income projections are. The ALM report will link these three strands across the group entity and also to each individual business line. That is, it will consider macro-level factors driving variations in interest income as well as specific desk-level factors. The former include changes in the shape and level of the yield curve, while the latter will include new business, customer behavior, and so on. Of necessity, the ALM report is a detailed, large document.

Table 8.2 is a summary overview of the responsibilities of the ALCO.

The ALCO must meet on a regular basis; the frequency depends on the type of institution but should be at least once a month. The composition of the ALCO also varies by institution but the norm is as described earlier. Representatives from the credit committee and loan syndication may also be present. A typical agenda would consider all the elements listed in Table 8.2. Thus the meeting will discuss and generate action points on the following:

- *Management reporting.* This will entail analyzing the various management reports and either signing off on them or agreeing on action items. The issues to consider include lending margin, interest income, variance from last projection, customer business, and future business. Current business policy with regard to lending and portfolio management will be reviewed and either continued or adjusted.

TABLE 8.2   ALCO Main Mission

Bank ALM Strategic Overview

Mission	Components
ALCO management and reporting	Formulating ALM strategy
	Management reporting
	ALCO agenda and minutes
	Assessing liquidity, gap, and interest-rate risk reports
	Scenario planning and analysis
	Interest income projection
Asset management	Managing bank liquidity book (CDs, bills)
	Managing Floating Rate Note book
	Investing bank capital
ALM strategy	Yield curve analysis
	Money market trading
Funding and liquidity management	Liquidity policy
	Managing funding and liquidity risk
	Ensuring funding diversification
	Managing lending of funds
Risk management	Formulating hedging policy
	Interest-rate risk exposure management
	Implementing hedging policy using cash and derivative instruments
Internal treasury function	Formulating transfer pricing system and level
	Funding group entities
	Calculating the cost of capital

- *Business planning.* Existing asset (and liability) books will be reviewed, and future business direction drawn up. This will consider the performance of existing business, most importantly with regard to return on capital. The existing asset portfolio will be analyzed from a risk/reward perspective, and a decision made to continue or modify all lines of business. Any proposed new business will be discussed and, if accepted in principle, will be moved on to the next stage.[11] At this stage any new business will be assessed for projected returns, revenue, and risk exposure.
- *Hedging policy.* Overall hedging policy will consider the acceptability of risk exposure, existing risk limits, and use of hedging instruments. The latter also includes use of derivative instruments. Many bank ALM desks find that their hedging requirements can be met using plain-vanilla products such as interest-rate swaps and exchange-traded short-

money futures contracts. The use of options, and even more vanilla derivative instruments such as forward rate agreements (FRAs), is much less common than one might think. Hedging policy takes into account the cash book revenue level, current market volatility levels, and the overall cost of hedging. On occasion certain exposures may be left unhedged because the costs associated with hedging them is deemed prohibitive (this includes the actual cost of putting on the hedge as well as the opportunity cost associated with expected reduced income from the cash book). Of course, hedging policy is formulated in coordination with overall funding and liquidity policy. Its final form must consider the bank's views of the following:

- Expectations on the future level and direction of interest rates.
- Balancing the need to manage and control risk exposure with the need to maximize revenue and income.
- Level of risk aversion, and how much risk exposure the bank is willing to accept.

The ALCO is dependent on management reporting from the ALM or treasury desk. The reports may be compiled by the treasury middle office. The main report is the overall ALM report, showing the composition of the bank's ALM book. Other reports look at specific business lines, and consider the return on capital generated by these businesses. These reports need to break down aggregate levels of revenue and risk by business line. Reports also drill down by product type, across business lines. Other reports consider the gap, the gap risk, the value at risk (VaR) or dollar value of one basis point (DV01) report, and credit risk exposures. Overall, the reporting system must be able to isolate revenues, return, and risk by country sector, business line, and product type. There is usually also an element of scenario planning, that is expected performance under various specified macro- and micro-level market conditions.

Figure 8.6 illustrates the general reporting concept.

ALCO REPORTING

We now provide a flavor of the reporting that is provided to, and analyzed by, the ALCO. This is a generalization; reports will, of course, vary by the type of the institution and the nature of its business.

Earlier we showed an example of a macro-level ALM report. The ALCO will also consider the macro-level gap and liquidity reports compiled for product and market. The interest-rate gap, being simply the difference

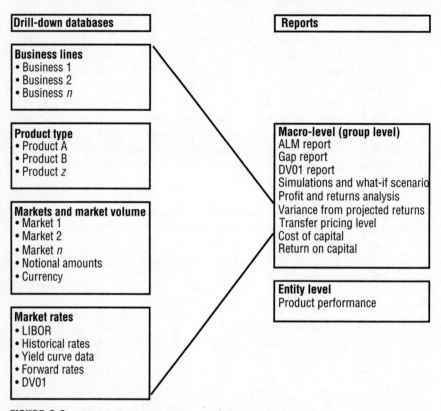

FIGURE 8.6   ALCO Reporting Input and Output

between assets and liabilities, is easily set into these parameters. For management reporting purposes the report will attempt to show a dynamic profile, but its chief limitation is that it is always a snapshot of a fixed point in time, and therefore, strictly speaking, will always be out-of-date.

Figure 8.7 shows a typical dynamic gap, positioned in a desired ALM smile, with the projected interest-rate gaps based on the current snapshot profile. This report shows future funding requirement, regarding which the ALCO can give direction that reflects their view on future interest rate levels. It also shows where the sensitivity to falling interest rates lies, in terms of revenue, because it shows the volume of assets. Again, the ALCO can give instructions on hedging if they expect interest income to be affected adversely. The x-axis is the time buckets from overnight out to two years or beyond. Banks use different time buckets to suit their own requirements.[12]

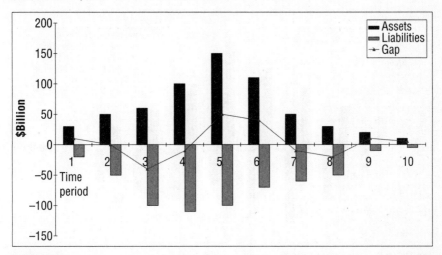

FIGURE 8.7 ALM and Expected Liquidity and Interest-Rate Gap, Snapshot Profile

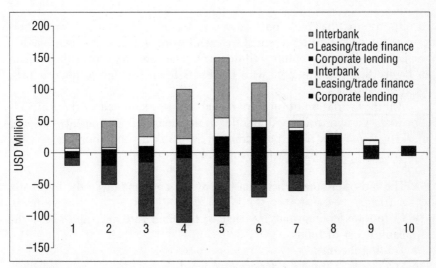

FIGURE 8.8 ALM Breakdown by Product (or Market) Segment

Figure 8.8 shows the same report with a breakdown by product (a report with a breakdown by market would have a similar layout). We use a hypothetical sample of different business lines. Using this format the ALCO can observe which assets and liabilities are producing the gaps, which is important because it shows whether products (or markets) are fitting into overall bank policy. Equally, policy can be adjusted if required

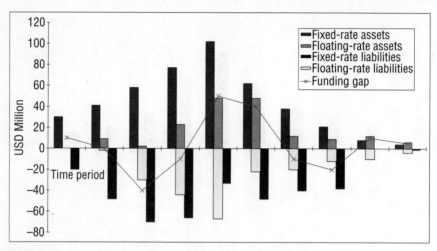

FIGURE 8.9   ALM Breakdown by Type of Interest Rate

in response to what the report shows. So the ALCO can see what proportion of total assets is represented by each business line, and which line has the greatest forward funding requirement. The same report is shown again in Figure 8.9, but this time with the breakdown by type of interest rate, fixed or variable.

Another variation of this report that will be examined by the ALCO is a breakdown by income and margin, again separated into business lines or markets as required. In a pure commercial banking operation the revenue type mix will comprise the following (among others):

- The bid-offer spread between borrowing and lending in the interbank market.
- Corporate lending margin—that is, the loan rate over and above the bank's cost of funds.
- Trading income.
- Fixed fees charged for services rendered.

The ALCO will receive an income breakdown report, split by business line. The x-axis in such a report would show the margin level for each time period—that is, it shows the margin of the lending rate over the cost of funds by each time bucket. Figure 8.10 is another type of income report, which shows the volumes and income spread by business line. The spread is shown in basis points and is an average for that time bucket (across

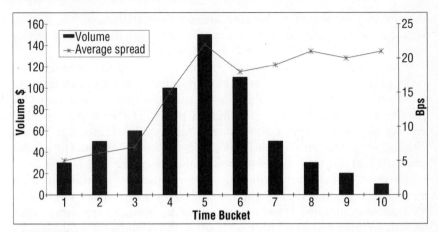

FIGURE 8.10   Asset Profile Volume and Average Income Spread

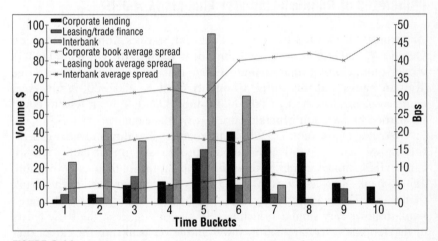

FIGURE 8.11   Business Lines and Average Income Spread

all loans and deposits for that bucket). The volumes will be those reported in the main ALM report (Figure 8.7) but this time with the margin contribution per time period. As we might expect, the spread levels per product across time are roughly similar; they will differ more markedly by product type. The latter report is shown in Figure 8.11.

Figure 8.11 is more useful because it shows the performance of each business line. In general, the ALCO will prefer low volumes and high margin as a combination, because lower volumes consume less capital. However, some significant high-volume business (such as interbank money market operations) operates at relatively low margin.

The income and return reports viewed by the ALCO are required in order to enable it to check whether bank policy with regard to lending and money market trading is being adhered to. Essentially these reports are providing information on the risk/return profile of the bank. The ideal combination is the lowest possible risk for the highest possible return, although of course low-risk business carries the lowest return. The level of trade-off that the bank is comfortable with is what the ALCO will set in its direction and strategy. With regard to volumes and bank business, it might be thought that the optimum mix is high-volume business mixed with high income margin. However, high-volume business consumes more capital, so there will be another trade-off with regard to use of capital.

PRINCIPLES OF BANKING LIQUIDITY RISK MANAGEMENT

At a conference hosted by the UK Financial Services Authority (FSA) on October 9, 2009, there was significant focus given to the UK bank HSBC's model of liquidity management.[13] Given that HSBC, rare among large Western banks, did not suffer a liquidity crisis in 2007–2009, observers commented on the efficacy of the HSBC model, and on what lessons could be learned by banks in general.

In truth, a close look at HSBC's approach to liquidity and asset generation shows that it is neither unique nor proprietary to that bank. The so-called HSBC model would have been the norm, rather than the exception, among banks as recently as 10 or 15 years ago (and in fact another bank that was largely unaffected by the 2008 bank crisis, Standard Chartered Bank, follows very similar principles). In an era of excess, the basic tenets of the approach were applied by fewer and fewer banks, to the extent that they were no longer seen as an essential ingredient of prudent bank risk management at the time of the 2007–2009 financial crash.

As such, these principles represent basic principles of banking, and not a specific response to the events of 2007–2009. They can be taken to be general principles of banking and liquidity risk management, and ones that more banks will readopt as they return to a more conservative business model, either through choice or because the requirements of the national banking regulator insist upon a more robust approach to risk management.

This section considers the most important principles of what should be taken to be nine cornerstones of banking and liquidity management.

1. *Fund illiquid assets with core customer deposits.* In hindsight, this looks like an eminently sensible guideline, but during the bull market buildup of 2001–2007 it was not applied universally. The best example of this was Northern Rock plc, which built an asset book that far exceeded its retail deposit base in size, but this pattern was observed with many banks in Western Europe. It is not difficult to ascertain the logic behind this principle: Core customer deposits are generally more stable than wholesale funds and also at lower risk of withdrawal in the event of a downturn in economic conditions (an apparent paradox is that they may actually increase as customers seek to deleverage and also hold off committing to cash-rich expenditures). Therefore, funding illiquid assets with core customer deposits is prudent banking practice.

2. *Where core customer deposits are not available, use long-term wholesale funding sources.* This follows naturally from the first principle. Where there are insufficient core deposits available, and banks resort to the wholesale funding market, banks should ensure that only long-dated wholesale funds are used to fund illiquid assets. Generally, *long-dated* means over one year in maturity, although of course the appropriate tenor to source is a function of the maturity of the asset. This approach reduces rollover liquidity risk in the event of a crisis.

3. *Do not overly rely on wholesale funding.* Run a sensible term structure wherever this is used: More funding should be in long-term (longer than five years) than in short-term. This follows from the primary dictum of not building up the asset base using wholesale funds unless absolutely necessary. Where recourse is made to wholesale funds, as much of this should be in the long term as possible, so as to minimize exposure to frequent short-term rollover risk to wholesale funds.

4. *Maintain liquidity buffers to handle stresses, both firm-specific and marketwide stresses.* The UK FSA has stipulated that this will be a requirement, in its *Policy Statement 09/16* published in October 2009. However, only 10 years ago it was quite common for banks to hold some of their assets in the form of liquidity-risk-free government bonds. Traditionally a bank's capital was always invested in such securities or in shorter-dated government bills, but beyond this it was accepted as good practice for banks to have a portion of their balance-sheet assets in sovereign securities. For the FSA to make it a requirement under law demonstrates the extent to which this practice fell into disuse.

   It is evident that banks reduced their holdings of government bonds so they could deploy more of their funds in higher-paying risky assets. But the logic of holding a liquidity buffer is irrefutable: In periods of stress or illiquidity, government bonds are the only assets that remain liquid. As such, if need be they can be sold to release liquidity. Even hitherto highly liquid assets such as high-rated bank CDs or short-dated medium-term notes (MTNs) became illiquid virtually overnight in the immediate aftermath of the Lehman collapse in 2008. This demonstrates that the liquidity buffer should be comprised of sovereign risk-free securities only.

5. *Establish a liquidity contingency plan.* A well-managed liquidity operation recognizes that bank funding should be sourced from multiple origins, and that *concentration risk* should be avoided both in any specific sector and to any one lender. However, even without excess concentration, at any time particular sectors or lenders may become unavailable, for either exogenous or endogenous reasons.

   Given this risk, banks need to have contingencies to fall back on whenever particular sources of funding dry up. This may include applying for and setting up facilities at the central bank, or establishing relationships with particular sectors that, for reasons of cost or convenience, the bank does not customarily access. The contingency plan needs to be tested regularly and kept updated.

6. *Know what central bank facilities the bank can assess and test access to them.* This follows logically from the requirement to have a contingency funding plan in place. Once a bank has established borrowing facilities at its central bank, it needs to be aware exactly how they function and what the requirements to access them are, so that if necessary it can benefit from them without delay.

7. *Be aware of all the bank's exposures (on the liability side, not credit side).* For example, sponsoring an asset-backed commercial paper (ABCP) conduit creates a reputational, rather than contractual, obligation to provide funding. Therefore, be aware of reputational obligations, especially if they mean the bank has to lend its name to another entity.

   This is fairly straightforward to understand, but in a bull market when credit spreads are tight it is frequently forgotten. Banks may desire the fee-based income, at favorable capital levels, that comes with sponsoring a third-party entity or providing a line of liquidity, but in a stress situation that line will be drawn on. Is the bank prepared to take on this additional liquidity risk exposure to an entity that it might not normally, in a bear market, wish to lend funds to?

8. *Use more than one metric.* Liquidity risk is not a single metric. It is an array of metrics, and a bank must calculate them all in order to obtain the most accurate picture of liquidity. This is especially true for multinational banks and/or banks with multiple business lines. Smaller banks often rely on just one or two liquidity indicators, such as loan-to-deposit ratio. Given that bank asset-liability management is more an

art than a science, it is vital that banks use a range of liquidity measures for risk estimation and forecasting. The next section addresses the different metrics required.

9. *The internal transfer pricing framework must be set correctly and adequately.* An artificial internal lending rate to business lines can drive inappropriate business decision making and was a factor behind the growth in risky assets during the buildup to the U.S. subprime crisis. We address this subject elsewhere in this chapter.

The business of banking is, if nothing else, the business of managing the gap between assets and liabilities. In the history of banking, banks have never matched their asset maturity with their funding liability maturity. But it is the management of this gap risk that should be the primary concern of all banks. The basic principles we have discussed here represent business best practice, evolved over centuries of modern banking, in mitigating gap risk.

MEASURING BANK LIQUIDITY RISK: KEY METRICS

As previously noted, given that bank asset-liability management is more an art than a science, it is vital that banks use a range of liquidity measures for risk estimation and forecasting. In this section we list six baseline liquidity metrics that all banks, irrespective of their size or line of business, should adopt and monitor as a matter of course. These are:

1. Loan-to-deposit ratio.
2. One-week and one-month liquidity ratios.
3. Cumulative liquidity model.
4. Liquidity risk factor.
5. Concentration report.
6. Inter-entity lending report.

These reports measure and illustrate different elements of liquidity risk. For consolidated or group banking entities, reports must be at country level, legal entity level, and group level. Taken together, on aggregate the reports provide detail on:

- The exposure of the bank to funding rollover or *gap* risk.
- The daily funding requirement, and what it is likely to be at a forward date.
- The extent of self-sufficiency of a branch or subsidiary.

Liquidity reports also help in providing early warning of any likely funding stress points. We examine them individually.

Loan-to-Deposit Ratio (LTD)

The LTD is the standard and commonly used metric, typically reported monthly. It measures the relationship between lending and customer deposits, and is a measure of the self-sustainability of the bank (or the branch or subsidiary). A level above 100 percent is an early warning sign of excessive asset growth; of course a level below 70 percent implies excessive liquidity and implies a potentially inadequate return on funds.

The LTD is a good measure of the contribution of customer funding to the bank's overall funding; however, it is not predictive and does not account for the tenor, concentration, and volatility of funds. As such, it is insufficient as a liquidity risk measure on its own and must be used in conjunction with the other measures.

One-Week and One-Month Liquidity Ratios

These are standard liquidity ratios that are commonly measured against a regulatory limit requirement. An example of a report for a group-type entity composed of four subsidiaries is shown in Table 8.3.

Liquidity ratios are an essential measure of gap risk. They show net cash flows, including the cash effect of liquidating liquid securities, as a percentage of liabilities, for a specific maturity bucket. These are an effective measure of structural liquidity, with early warning of likely stress points.

A more detailed liquidity ratio report is shown in Table 8.4. This shows the breakdown of cash inflows and outflows per time bucket, and also the

TABLE 8.3   Sample Liquidity Ratio Report

Country	One-Week Gap	One-Week Liquidity		One-Month Liquidity	
	USD mm	This Week Limit	Excess	This Week Limit	Excess
F	−1,586	−22.83%	−30.00%	−39.11%	−50.00%
D	188	15.26%	0.00%	1.62%	−5.00%
H	786	22.57%	0.00%	19.12%	−5.00%
G	550	53.27%	25.00%	69.83%	25.00%
Regional Total	−62	−0.48%		−10.64%	

TABLE 8.4 Liquidity Report and Liquidity Ratio Calculation

EURO

XYZ Bank, London—Liquidity Report
November 28, 2009

	Sight	2–8 Days	9 Days–1 Month	1–3 Months	3–6 Months	6 Months to 1 Year	1–3 Years	3–5 Years	>5 Years	Total
Corporate current/call	24,289	0	0	0	0	0	0	0	0	24,289
Corporate time loan	28,433	14,203	151,471	106,637	98,959	47,608	357,872	573,993	642,563	2,021,738
Government current/call	342	0	0	0	0	0	0	0	0	342
Government time loan	250	3	805	63	3,383	2,942	12,656	7,016	76,853	103,971
Interbank current/call	41,752	0	0	0	0	0	0	0	0	41,752
Interbank time loan	339,276	201,745	6,251	31,906	18,704	28,428	11,971	0	0	638,281
Repos	0	0	47,500	0	0	0	0	0	0	47,500
Intergroup current/call	4,445	0	0	0	0	0	0	0	0	4,445
Intergroup time loan	210,177	348,414	277,964	76,268	13,981	30,047	156	101	0	957,108
Marketable securities and CDs—<1 month to maturity	5,009	0	55,358	0	0	0	0	0	0	60,367
Retail current/call	8,215	0	0	0	0	0	0	0	0	8,215
Retail time loan	238	41	221	2,643	2,427	310	6,294	38,755	10,204	61,133
Additional corporate time lending	0	8	1,313	43	624	0	21,608	7,857	75,724	107,177
Receivables	0	0	0	0	0	0	0	0	0	0
Total Assets	662,426	564,414	493,383	265,060	138,078	109,335	410,557	627,722	805,344	4,076,318
Corporate current/call	51,033	0	0	12,758	0	0	0	0	0	63,791
Corporate time deposit	32,303	122,955	114,627	299,551	28,387	928	0	0	0	598,751
Government current/call	1,946	0	0	0	0	0	0	0	0	1,946
Government time deposit	2,056	8,112	24,391	23,503	22,687	1,200	0	0	0	81,949
Interbank current/call	82,087	0	0	0	0	0	0	0	0	82,087
Interbank time deposit	83,898	83,684	349,461	86,979	23,967	1,205	0	0	0	629,194
Repos	0	0	50,000	0	0	0	0	0	0	50,000
Intergroup current/call	47,095	0	0	0	0	0	0	0	0	47,095
Intergroup time deposit	302,879	418,383	629,809	225,314	88,464	78,769	375	0	0	1,743,993
Retail current/call	65,273	0	16,318	0	0	0	0	0	0	81,591
Retail time deposit	203	54,128	167,090	683,288	27,925	13,273	9,224	0	0	955,131
Additional government/local authority time deposits	8,656	9,319	50,508	82,531	15,252	8,500	1,000	0	0	175,766
Share capital	0	0	0	0	0	0	0	0	0	0
Payables	0	0	0	0	0	0	0	0	0	0
Total Liabilities	677,429	696,581	1,335,886	1,480,242	206,682	103,875	10,599	0	0	4,511,294

Ratio Calculation	Sight	Sight—8 Days	Sight—1 M
Marketable securities	0	630,536	630,536
Repos Adjusted	0	0	0
CD's GBP denominated 39,000	0	353,219	353,219
Unutilized gains	(55,520)	(55,520)	(55,520)
Liquidity gap	(13,603)	(147,170)	(969,673)
Total available funds	(70,523)	781,065	(61,438)
Total liabilities	4,511,294	4,511,294	4,511,294

Liquidity Ratio	-1.56%	17.31%	-1.36%
	45	45	45
Internal limit	3.00%	3.00%	-3.00%
FSA limit	0.00%	0.00%	-5.00%

Stress testing	10% fall in marketable securities	15.13%	-3.54%
Stress testing	10% fall in stickiness	17.32%	-2.79%
Stress testing	Combined effect of above	15.14%	-4.97%

Liquidity gap is assets minus liabilities in relevant tenor bucket

Total available funds is liquidity gap, plus marketable securities (FRNs), CDs and committed facilities that are as yet undrawn (which is subtracted)

4,511,294   434,976   TOTAL ALM GAP ALL TENORS

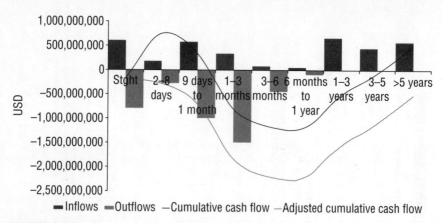

FIGURE 8.12   Cumulative Liquidity Model

liquidity ratio. The ratio itself is calculated by dividing the selected time bucket liability by the cumulative liability. So in this example the 30-day ratio of 17.3 percent is given by the fraction 781,065/4,511,294.

Cumulative Liquidity Model

The cumulative liquidity model is an extension of the liquidity ratio report and is a forward-looking model of inflows, outflows, and available liquidity, accumulated for a 12-month period. It recognizes and predicts liquidity stress points on a cash basis. A report such as this, like the liquidity ratios, will be prepared daily at legal entity level and group level.

Figure 8.12 is an example of a cumulative outflow graph rising from the cumulative liquidity model. It gives a snapshot view of forward-funding stress points.

Liquidity Risk Factor (LRF)

This measure shows the aggregate size of the liquidity gap: It compares the average tenor of assets to the average tenor of liabilities. It is also known as a *maturity transformation report*. The ratio can be calculated using years or days, as desired. For example, Table 8.5 is an example of the risk factor for a hypothetical bank, where the unit of measurement is days. In this example, the ratio 262/19 is slightly below 14.

The higher the LRF, the larger the liquidity gap, and the greater the liquidity risk.

TABLE 8.5 Liquidity Risk Factor

Report Date	Average Liabilities Tenor (days)	Average Assets Tenor (days)	Maturity Transformation Effect	Limit
03/09/2009	19	262	14	24

TABLE 8.6 Large Depositors as a Percentage of Total Funding Report

Customer	Deposit Amount ($000s)	Percentage of Banking Funding	Percentage of Group External Funding
Customer 1	836,395	17.1%	2.6%
Customer 2	595,784	7.9%	1.8%
Customer 3	425,709	5.8%	1.3%
Customer 4	241,012	0.6%	0.7%
Customer 6	214,500	1.2%	0.7%
Customer 21	190,711	4.5%	0.6%
Customer 17	123,654	2.9%	0.4%
Customer 18	97,877	2.3%	0.3%
Customer 14	89,344	2.1%	0.3%
Customer 15	88,842	2.1%	0.3%
Customer 31	83,272	2.0%	0.3%
Customer 19	74,815	0.5%	0.2%
Customer 10	64,639	1.5%	0.2%
Customer 29	59,575	1.4%	0.2%
Customer 16	58,613	1.4%	0.2%
Total	6,562,116	53.3%	20.1%

It is important to observe the trend over time and the change to long-run averages, so as to get early warning of the buildup of a potentially unsustainable funding structure.

Concentration Report and Funding Source Report

This report shows the extent of reliance on single sources of funds. An excess concentration with any one lender, sector, or country is an early-warning sign of potential stress points in the event of a crash event.

An example of a concentration report is shown in Table 8.6. In this example, Customer 1 is clearly the focus of a potential stress point, and a bank would need to put in a contingency in the event that this source of funds dries up.

A related report is the funding source report, an example of which is shown in Table 8.7. This is a summary of the share of funding obtained from all the various sources, and should be used to flag potential concentration risk by sector.

Interentity Lending Report

This report is relevant for group and consolidated banking entities. As intra-group lending is common in banking entities, this report is a valuable tool used to determine how reliant a specific banking subsidiary is on group funds. An example of a report for a group entity is shown in Table 8.8.

TABLE 8.7   Funding Source Report

Source	Balance (€000,000s)	Percentage of Funding	Limit	Limit Breach (Y/N)
Corporate and retail customer	1,891	46%	> 40%	Y
Institutional financial institutions	675	17%	< 25% or 1 billion	Y
Interbank	301	7%	< 25% or 1 billion	Y
Inter-group (net balance)	400	10%	< 25% or 1 billion	Y
Other	20	0%	< 25% or 1 billion	Y
Total liabilities	4,087			

TABLE 8.8   Sample Intercompany Lending Report

Group Treasury

As of (date)	Total Borrowing	Total Lending	Net Intergroup Lending
London	1,713,280	883,133	−830,157
Paris	3,345,986	978,195	−2,367,617
Frankfurt	17,026	195,096	178,089
Dublin	453,490	83,420	−370,070
Hong Kong	0	162,000	162,000
New York	690,949	1,516,251	825,302

We have described the range of reports that represent essential metrics in the measurement of liquidity risk. They are the minimum management information that banks and group treasuries will wish to prepare, both as business best practice and as part of adherence to new regulatory standards.

INTERNAL FUNDING RATE POLICY

We define *liquidity risk* as the risk of being unable to (1) raise funds to meet payment obligations as they fall due and (2) fund an increase in assets. *Funding risk* is the risk of being unable to borrow funds in the market. The United Kingdom regulatory authority, the FSA, has prescribed a mechanism to mitigate liquidity and funding risk that is notable for its focus on the type, tenor, source, and availability of funding, exercised in normal and stressed market conditions.[14]

This emphasis on liquidity is correct, and an example of a return to the roots of banking, when liquidity management was paramount. While capital ratios are a necessary part of bank risk management, they are not sufficient. Northern Rock and Bradford & Bingley were more a failure of liquidity management than a matter of capital erosion. Hence, it is not surprising that there is now a strong focus on the extraneous considerations to funding.

However, the use of that funding within banks, including the price at which cash is internally lent or transferred to business lines, has not been as closely scrutinized by the FSA. This issue needs to be addressed by regulators because it is a driver of bank business models, which were shown to be flawed and based on inaccurate assumptions during 2007–2009.

An Effective Internal Funding Framework

While the FSA does touch on bank internal liquidity pricing,[15] the coverage is peripheral. This is unfortunate, because it is a key element driving a bank's business model. Essentially, the price at which an individual bank business line raises funding from its treasury desk is a major parameter in business decision making, driving sales, asset allocation, and product pricing. It is also a key hurdle rate behind the product approval process and in an individual business line's performance measurement. Just as capital allocation decisions affecting front-office business units need to account for the cost of that capital (in terms of return on regulatory and economic capital), so funding decisions exercised by corporate treasurers carry significant implications for sales and trading teams at the trade level.

In an ideal world, the price at which cash is internally transferred within a bank should reflect the true economic cost of that cash (at each maturity band), and its impact on overall bank liquidity. This would ensure that each business aligns the commercial propensity to maximize profit with the correct maturity profile of associated funding. From a liquidity point of view, any mismatch between the asset tenor and funding tenor, after taking into account the repossession ability of each asset class in question, should be highlighted and acted upon as a matter of priority, with the objective to reduce recourse to short-term, passive funding as much as possible. Equally, it is important that the internal funding framework be transparent to all trading groups.

A measure of discipline in business decision making is enforced via the imposition of minimum ROC targets. Independent of the internal cost of funds, a business line would ordinarily seek to ensure that any transaction it entered into achieved its targeted ROC. However, relying solely on this measure is not always sufficient discipline. For this to work, each business line should first be set ROC levels that are commensurate with its (risk-adjusted) risk/reward profile. However, banks do not always set different target ROCs for each business line, which means that the required discipline breaks down. Second, a uniform cost of funds, even allowing for different ROCs, will mean that the different liquidity stresses created by different types of assets are not addressed adequately at the aggregate funding level.

For example, consider the following asset types:

- Three-month interbank loan.
- Three-year floating-rate corporate loan, fixing quarterly.
- Three-year floating-rate corporate loan, fixing weekly.
- Three-year fixed-rate loan.
- Ten-year floating-rate corporate loan, fixing monthly.
- Fifteen-year floating-rate project finance loan, fixing quarterly.

We have selected these asset types deliberately, to demonstrate the different liquidity pressures that each places on the treasury funding desk (listed in increasing amount of funding rollover risk). Even allowing for different credit risk exposures and capital risk weights, the impact on the liability funding desk is different for each asset. We see then the importance of applying a structurally sound transfer pricing policy, dependent on the type of business line being funded.

Cost of Funds

As a key driver of the economic decision-making process, the cost at which funds are lent from the central treasury to the bank's businesses needs to be set at a rate that reflects the true liquidity risk position of each business line. If it is unrealistic, there is a risk that transactions are entered into that produce an unrealistic profit. This profit will reflect the artificial funding gain, rather than the true economic value-added of the business.

There is empirical evidence of the damage that can be caused by artificially low transfer pricing. In a paper from 2008, Adrian Blundell-Wignall and Paul Atkinson[16] discuss the losses at UBS AG in its structured credit business, which originated and invested in collateralized debt obligations (CDOs). They quote a UBS shareholder report:

> *. . . internal bid prices were always higher than the relevant London inter-bank bid rate (LIBID) and internal offer prices were always lower than relevant London inter-bank offered rate (LIBOR).*

In other words, UBS's structured credit business was able to fund itself at prices better than in the market (which is implicitly interbank risk), despite the fact that it was investing in assets of considerably lower liquidity (and credit quality) than interbank risk. There was no adjustment for tenor mismatch, to better align term funding to liquidity. A more realistic funding model was viewed as a "constraint on the growth strategy."

This lack of funding discipline undoubtedly played an important role in the decision-making process, because it allowed the desk to report inflated profits based on low funding costs. As a stand-alone business, a CDO investor would not expect to raise funds at sub-LIBOR, but rather at significantly over LIBOR. By receiving this artificial low pricing, the desk could report super profits and very high ROC, which encouraged more and more risky investment decisions.

Another example involved banks that entered into the *fund derivatives* business. This was lending to investors in hedge funds via a leveraged structured product. These instruments were illiquid, with maturities of two years or longer. Once dealt, they could not be unwound, thus creating significant liquidity stress for the lender. However, banks funded these business lines from the central treasury at LIBOR-flat, rolling short-term. The liquidity problems that resulted became apparent during the 2007–2009 financial crisis, when interbank liquidity dried up.

Many banks operate on a similar model, with a fixed internal funding rate of LIBOR plus, say, 15 basis points (bps) for all business lines, and for any tenor. But such an approach does not take into account the differing risk/reward and liquidity profiles of the businesses. The corporate lending desk will create different liquidity risk exposures for the bank compared to the CDO desk or the project finance desk. For the most efficient capital allocation, banks should adjust the basic internal transfer price for the resulting liquidity risk exposure of the business. Otherwise they run the risk of excessive risk taking heavily influenced by an artificial funding gain.

Business Best Practice

It is important that the regulatory authorities review the internal funding structure in place at the banks they supervise. An artificially low funding rate can create as much potentially unmanageable risk exposure as a risk-seeking loan origination culture. A regulatory requirement to impose a realistic internal funding arrangement will mitigate this risk.

We recommend the following approach: a fixed add-on spread over LIBOR for term loans or assets over a certain maturity, say one year, where the coupon refix is frequent (such as weekly or monthly), to compensate for the liquidity mismatch. The spread would be on a sliding scale for longer-term assets.

Internal funding discipline is as pertinent to bank risk management as capital buffers and effective liquidity management discipline. As banks adjust to the new liquidity requirements soon to be imposed by the FSA, it is worth their looking beyond the literal scope of the new supervisory fiat to consider the internal determinants of an efficient, cost-effective funding regime. In this way they can move toward the heart of this proposition, which is to embed true funding cost into business-line decision making.

Funds Transfer Pricing Policy: Liquidity Premium Framework

This policy framework is recommended to better reflect the usage and provision of funds that flow through the treasury as a result of the business undertaken by the individual bank business lines (strategic business units, or SBUs). It is meant to be reflective of market conditions and is separate from any treasury margin that may be applied.

It is also a requirement of the UK FSA under *Policy Statement 09/16* that the cost of liquidity should be included as part of the internal pricing of funds within an entity. We refer to this internal funding rate as the *transfer price* (TP). TP does not in any way reflect credit spread or credit premium. It is a pure liquidity premium.

Scope

This policy applies to all interest-bearing assets and liabilities on the bank's balance sheet. It includes:

- All interest-bearing assets and liabilities that are *live*.
- The separate trading desks within the Treasury.
- The gross cash flows of each SBU or trading desk. Per the existing transfer pricing rules for interest-rate risk, there is no netting allowed by the SBUs.
- Non-interest-bearing assets and liabilities are covered under a separate policy.

Framework

The TP policy applies equally to both sides of the balance sheet.

Assets   The proposed framework for the pricing of assets is as follows:

- LIBOR will be used as the basis for funding as per existing transfer pricing rules.
- The final maturity date for assets is to be determined by reference to the shorter of economic life or legal maturity date. Economic life, in the case of corporate lending/securities, is to be determined on a case-by-case basis, although legal maturity date is to be used as the default end point.
- Pricing applies to legacy trades as set out under the preceding subsection titled "Scope."
- The pricing framework has been set by the treasury and agreed to by the bank's ALCO as follows:

Period to Maturity	Less than 6 Months	6–12 Months	1–5 Years	Longer than 5 Years
Assets	LIBOR	LIBOR + 4 bps	LIBOR + 8 bps	LIBOR + 12 bps

Liabilities   The proposed framework for the pricing of liabilities is as follows:

- LIBOR will be used as the basis for funding as per existing transfer pricing rules.
- The final maturity date for liabilities is to be determined by reference to the longer of economic life or final maturity date. Economic life will be determined with reference to the stickiness rate allowed by the FSA under current reporting rules:

Corporate deposits	50 percent
Retail deposits	60 percent

- For the purposes of this framework, deposits that have had stickiness applied will be treated as having an economic life of one to five years. Stickiness is applied on a portfolio basis.
- Pricing applies to legacy trades as set out under the preceding subsection titled "Scope."
- The pricing framework has been set by the treasury and agreed by ALCO as follows:

Period to Maturity	Less than 6 Months	6–12 Months	1–5 Years	Longer than 5 Years
Liabilities	LIBOR	LIBOR + 4 bps	LIBOR + 8 bps	LIBOR + 12 bps

Ongoing

On an ongoing basis:

- The ALCO is responsible for ensuring that this policy is maintained.
- A review of the pricing framework is to be undertaken by the ALCO every six months.
- Pricing can be updated more frequently should market conditions require it.

Calculation Methodology: The Liquidity Premium

The TP rate will be reviewed every six months to ensure that it is realistic to the market. There is no universal method to calculate the liquidity premium that should be added to the LIBOR funding cost.

Approaches include:

- The difference between asset swap (ASW) and credit default swap (CDS) of the banks (where this is negative) for each tenor maturity.
- The difference between the funding spread over a bank of the same credit rating.
- A subjective add-on based on what the ALCO believes the bank will pay to raise longer-dated funds, separate from the credit risk perception of the bank.

- The difference between the funded and unfunded rates for that bank (its swap pay-fixed rate against its bond fixed rate of the same tenor)
- The difference between the pay-fixed rate on the term swap and the pay-fixed rate on the same maturity overnight-index swap (OIS).

In practice, an average number calculated from all the approaches above is likely to be used.

CONCLUSION

In this chapter we have considered the essential principles of bank asset-liability management, and the main tenets of bank liquidity risk management. The events of 2007–2009 served to reiterate the importance of sound ALM practice in banks. For this reason it is important that a bank's ALCO be set up as an effective management entity at every bank, empowered to ensure correct business practice for asset-liability management. The framework set out in this chapter can be viewed as the best-endeavors approach to the operation of the ALCO function at a bank.

CHAPTER 9

A Sustainable Bank Business Model: Capital, Liquidity, and Leverage

The global financial crisis has had the effect of making all participants in the banking industry—from regulators, central banks, and governments to bank boards, directors, and trade associations—take a fundamental look at the principles of banking. Issues such as capital and liquidity management and systemic risk became the subject of renewed focus. In practical terms, legislators realized that they needed to address the issue of the too-big-to-fail bank, and this issue remains unresolved.

From the point of view of bank practitioners, the most important task is to address the issues of capital, liquidity, and risk management and work them into a coherent strategy that is designed to produce sustainable returns over the business cycle. In this chapter we discuss these topics and consider how bank strategy can be formulated to handle the changed requirements of the post-crisis age. The contents are laid out as follows:

- Bank business models
- Corporate governance
- Liqudity risk management
- Liquidity asset buffer

We list recommendations for the new banking approach in the conclusion at the end of this chapter.

THE NEW BANK BUSINESS MODEL

The basic bank business model has remained unchanged since banks were first introduced in modern society. Of course, as it as much art as science, the model parameters themselves can be set to suit the specific strategy of the individual bank, depending on whether the strategy operates at a higher or lower risk/reward profile. But the basic model is identical across all banks. In essence, banking involves taking risks, and then the effective management of that risk. This risk can be categorized as follows:

- Managing the bank's capital.
- Managing the liquidity mismatch. A fundamental ingredient of banking is *maturity transformation*, the recognition that loans (assets) generally have a longer tenor than deposits (liabilities).

If we wished to summarize the basic ingredients of the historical bank model, we might describe it in the following terms:

- Leverage: A small capital base is levered up into an asset pool that can be 10, 20, 30 times greater, or even higher.
- The gap: essentially funding short to lend long. The gap is a function of the conventional positively sloping yield curve, and dictated by the recognition of the asset-liability mismatch previously noted.
- Liquidity: an assumption that a bank will always be able to roll over funding as it falls due.
- Risk management: an understanding of credit or default risk.

These fundamentals remain unchanged. The critical issue for bank management, however, is that some of the assumptions behind the application of these fundamentals *have* changed, as demonstrated by the crash of 2007–2009. The changed landscape in the wake of the crisis has resulted in some hitherto seemingly safe or profitable business lines being viewed as risky. Although favorable conditions for banking may well return in due course, for the foreseeable future the challenge for banks will be to set their strategy only after first arriving at a true and full understanding of economic conditions as they exist today. The first subject for discussion is to consider what a realistic, sustainable return on capital target level should be, and that it is commensurate with the level of risk aversion desired by the board. The board should also consider the bank's capital availability, and what sustained amount of business this would realistically support. These two issues need to be addressed before the remainder of the bank's strategy can be considered.

Bank Strategy

The most important function that a bank board can undertake is to set the bank's strategy. This is not as obvious as it sounds. It may be surprising to a layperson to see how often banks, both large and small, both sophisticated and plain vanilla, have no real articulated strategy, but this is a fact. What is vital is that banks have in place a coherent, articulated strategy that sets the tone for the entire business, from the top down.

In the first instance the board must take into account the current regulatory environment. This includes the requirements of the forthcoming Basel III rules. A bank cannot formulate strategy without a clear understanding of the environment in which it operates. Once this is achieved, before proceeding with a formal strategy the bank needs to determine in what markets it wishes to operate, with what products, and for what class of customer. All its individual business lines should be set up to operate within the main strategy, having identified the markets and customers.

In other words, a bank cannot afford to operate by simply meandering along, noting its peer group market share and return on equity (ROE), and making up strategy as it goes along. This approach, which again is evidently what many banks do indeed follow, however inadvertently, results in a senior management and board that are not fully aware of what the bank's liabilities and risk exposures are.

The first task is to understand one's operating environment, and then to incorporate a specific target market and product suite as the basis of its strategy. Concurrent with this, the bank must set its ROE target, which drives much of the bank's culture and ethos. It is important to get this part of the process right and at the start. Prior to the recent crash, it was common for banks to seek to increase revenue by adding to their risk exposure. Assets were added to the balance sheet or higher risk assets were taken on. In the bull market environment of 2001–2007, and allied to low funding costs as a result of low base interest rates, this resulted in ever higher ROE figures, to the point where it was common for even Tier 2 banks to target levels of 22 to 25 percent ROE in their business appraisal. This process was, of course, not tenable in the long run.

The second task, following immediately from the first, is to set a realistic ROE target and one that is sustainable over the entire business cycle. This cannot be done without educating board directors as well as shareholders, who must appreciate the new, lower ROE targets. Managing expectations will contribute to a more dispassionate review of strategy. As importantly, risk-adjusted ROE should also be set at a realistic level and not be allowed to increase. Hence, the board and shareholders must accept that lower ROE levels will become the standard. This should also be allied to lower leverage levels and higher capital ratios.

Concurrently with this process, a bank must also ask itself where its strength lies, and formulate its strategy around that. In other words, it is important to focus on core competencies. Again, the experience of the crash has served to demonstrate that many banks found themselves exposed to risk exposures that they did not understand. This may have been simply the holding of assets (such as structured finance securities) whose credit exposures, valuation, and secondary market liquidity they did not understand, or embarking on investment strategies such as negative basis trading without being aware of all the measurement parameters of such strategies.[1] To properly implement a coherent, articulate strategy, a bank needs to be aware of exactly what it does and does not have an expertise for undertaking, and not operate in products or markets in which it has no genuine knowledge base.

Allied to an understanding of core competence is a review of core and noncore assets. Bank strategy is not a static process or document, but rather a dynamic process. Regular reviews of the balance sheet need to be undertaken to identify any noncore assets, which can then be assessed to determine whether they remain compatible with the strategy. If they are not, then a realistic disposal process would need to be drawn up. In the long run, this is connected with an understanding of where the bank's real strengths lie. Long-term core assets may well differ from core assets, but this needs to be articulated explicitly. The decision of whether an asset is core or noncore, or core or long-term core, is a function of the bank's overall strategy of what its expertise is and what markets and customers it wishes to serve. These decisions will be embedded in the strategy and the bank's business model. This drives the choice of products and business lines that the bank feels it can add value in.

Leverage Ratios

Elsewhere we discuss bank capital structure. There is no doubt that the new model for banking assumes higher capital ratios and buffers for all banks during the next 10 years. The higher level of capital will be substantial in some cases, because under the proposed Basel III rules, trading businesses will be required to hold up to three times as much capital as vanilla banking businesses. It is also evident that many bank jurisdictions will, in addition, implement leverage ratio limits.

A *leverage ratio* is the total value of a bank's assets relative to its equity capital. The financial crash highlighted the extent of risk taking by certain banks when measured using leverage ratios. As a measure of the ratio of assets to owner's equity, they are an explicit indication of risk exposure. Lehman Brothers' leverage ratio increased from approximately 24:1 in 2003 to over 31:1 by 2007. Such aggressive asset growth generated tremendous profits during the boom years, but exposed the bank to such an extent that even a 3 or 4 percent decline in the value of its assets would completely eliminate its equity. This duly happened.

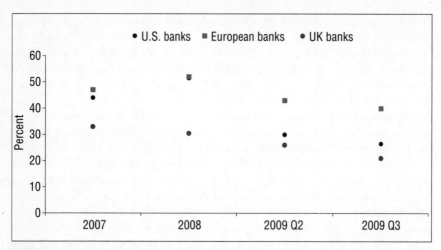

FIGURE 9.1   Bank Median Leverage Ratios, 2007–2009
Source: Bank of England (2009)

The Basel Committee for Banking Supervision (BCBS), as well as some national regulatory authorities, will introduce a limit on leverage ratios as an added safety measure alongside capital requirements. In the aftermath of the crash it is accepted that bank leverage ratios have to adjust downward, and the prevailing sentiment today dictates that boards should be wary of a business model that ramps up the ratio to an excessive level. Figure 9.1 shows levels during 2007–2009; prudent management suggests average levels will be much lower than these figures during the next 10 to 15 years. Not only is this business best practice, but lower average leverage ratio levels will also contribute to greater systemic stability.

Bank management will have to adjust to a concept of an explicit ratio limit, the rationale for which is clear. The experience of the recent and previous crises has shown that during a period of upside growth, banks' risk models tend to underestimate their exposure. This has two consequences: (1) The bank takes on ever greater risk, as it targets greater revenue and profit during a bull market, and (2) the amount of capital set aside is below what is adequate at the time the crash occurs.

Figure 9.2, which shows a sample of bulge-bracket banks, suggests that banks focused on trading assets as they expanded their balance sheets. In such an environment, capital ratio requirements are an insufficient safeguard against instability, and it becomes necessary to monitor leverage ratios. Hence, in the post-crash environment banks need to adjust their business strategy to allow for this constraint.

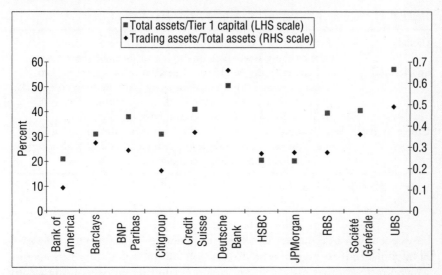

FIGURE 9.2 Selected Bank Ratios of Total Assets to Tier 1 Capital and Trading Assets to Total Assets
Source: Bank of England (2009).

As we noted earlier in the case of Lehman Brothers, excessively high leverage results in a higher sensitivity of the balance sheet to trading and/ or default losses. Limiting the amount of leverage acts as an additional risk control measure, backing up the safety net provided by a regulatory capital buffer. In advance of the introduction of a standardized ratio, as part of a future Basel III, banks can address this issue themselves as part of their prudential capital and risk management.

Note that a number of jurisdictions already employ a leverage ratio limit, although there is no uniform definition (see Table 9.1). It is likely that the new Basel III rules will incorporate a limit, with a common definition of capital and an agreed measure of all assets, both on- and off-balance-sheet.

Capital Structure

The efficient management of capital is a vital function of bank senior management. In the aftermath of any recession, capital is of course a scarce commodity. However, this fact itself leads to one of the lessons learned from the crisis: the need for *countercyclical* capital management. In other words, boards should treat capital as scarce at all times, and build up capital

TABLE 9.1   Summary of Selected Regulatory Leverage Ratio Limits

Canada	Tier 1 and Tier 2 capital must be at least 5 percent of on-balance-sheet assets plus qualifying off-balance-sheet assets.
Switzerland	Tier 1 capital must be at least 3 percent of on-balance-sheet assets less Swiss domestic lending for bank holding companies, and at least 4 percent for individual institutions. This rule applies only to Credit Suisse and UBS.
United States	Tier 1 capital must be at least 3 percent of on-balance-sheet assets for strong bank holding companies and at least 4 percent for all other bank holding companies.

Source: Bank of England (2009).

bases even as a bull market is helping to generate higher profits. The level of capital needs to be sufficient to cushion the fallout from *stress events*, which are the outlier events that normal distribution models of finance do not capture.

Elsewhere in this book we have discussed the value of contingent capital instruments that can convert to equity at any time that the issuing bank's capital ratio falls below a prespecified level. Going forward, this should be the only sophisticated financial instrument in the bank's capital structure. It will assist efficient capital management, as well as investor transparency, if a bank's capital is held in the form of simple instruments only, essentially common equity and retained profits (reserves). Of course, long-dated debt instruments can also form part of capital, but again it is more transparent if these are vanilla instruments.

Capital itself on its own is an insufficient protection against firm failure. This is why bank management must take additional measures, over and above capital buffers, to safeguard the institution in the event of systemic stress or other market crash events, because the capital base on its own will be insufficient to preserve the firm as a going concern. Hence, leverage ratio limits and robust liquidity management are as important as capital buffers. A report from the Bank of England (2009) has suggested that on average, a Tier 1 capital ratio of 8.5 percent would have been needed by banks if they were to avoid falling below the Basel II minimum of 4 percent during the last crisis. This suggests that the current requirement is far too low to act as a genuine risk-based capital reserve. Of course, a financial crisis will affect different banks in different ways; the Bank of England (BoE) report goes on to state that even if all the banks in its study sample had indeed possessed a Tier 1 ratio of 8.5 percent, as many as 40 percent of those

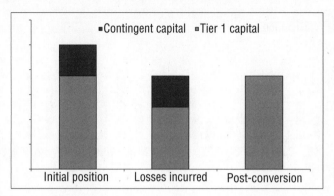

FIGURE 9.3   Illustration of Contingent Capital Note Triggering
Source: Bank of England (2009).

banks would still have breached their 4 percent limit during the crash. For some firms the sufficient level of capital acknowledged in hindsight was as high as 18 percent.

The implications of the BoE report are clear: Minimum capital requirements must be higher, and banks also need to build an element of flexibility into their capital structure, perhaps by means of the contingent capital instruments we discussed in Chapter 5. Contingent capital is any instrument that would convert into common equity at the occurrence of a prespecified trigger. This is illustrated in Figure 9.3. An issue of bonds by Lloyds Banking Group in 2009, Enhanced Capital Notes, was of this type. Such instruments enable a bank to purchase catastrophe insurance from the private sector rather than from the public sector via the lender of last resort. They also allow a bank to hold a Tier 1 equity reserve at a lower cost, in theory at least, than equity itself.

Core Competence: Know Your Risk

Regulatory authorities noticed a considerable decline in cross-border lending flows in the aftermath of the Lehman bankruptcy (for instance, see the Bank of England's *Financial Stability Report* dated June 2009). This is significant. During the bull market of 2001–2007, international lending volumes had expanded steadily (see Figure 9.4), as banks grew their balance sheets and sought higher yield opportunities elsewhere.

It is evident that during and after the bank crisis, when interbank market liquidity had dried up, banks pulled back from overseas markets,

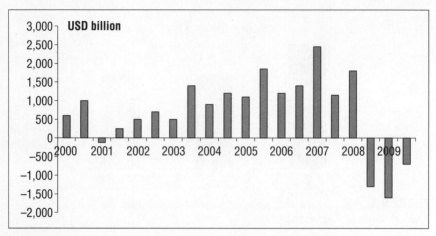

FIGURE 9.4   Cross-Border Bank Lending Volumes, 2000–2009
Source: Bank of England (2009).

irrespective of whether these were deemed peripheral, and concentrated on core markets. This reflects informational advantages in core markets compared to overseas and noncore markets. The UK corporate lending sector makes a case in point: Between 2002 and 2009, lending volume from UK banks fell by approximately 16 percent (the figure between 2006 and 2009 was a decline of 14 percent). However, the equivalent figures for foreign subsidiaries was a fall of 10.5 percent and 20 percent while for foreign branches the decline was even more dramatic, at 17 percent and 46 percent.[2] Foreign banks would, on average, have less depth and breadth of corporate relationships, while branches would be expected to have even less developed relationships in the domestic market.

The lessons for the bank business model are clear: During an expansionary phase, it is important to remain focused on areas of core competence and sectors in which the bank possesses actual knowledge and strength. Concentrating on areas in which the bank carries a competitive advantage makes it less likely that loan origination standards will decline, resulting in lower losses during an economic downturn. There is also a technical reason for ensuring that overseas lending standards are maintained strictly, and limits set carefully, because it is often undertaken in foreign currency. A bank's ability to fund such lending is more dependent on external markets and wholesale counterparties relative to domestic lending, thus making the bank more vulnerable to a market downturn. For example, the cross-currency swap market in U.S. dollars came under pressure, resulting in higher swap prices, following the Lehman default, and many banks struggled to obtain dollar funding.

CORPORATE GOVERNANCE

The governance structure of the bank is a vital part of ensuring effective overall control and risk management. An inadequate setup will result in ineffective decision making. The recent crash has highlighted the importance of addressing in robust fashion the following:

- What should the makeup of the board itself be? What is the right number of executive directors and nonexecutive directors (NEDs)?
- How should the performance of the board be measured?
- Are the knowledge base, expertise, and experience of the board adequate? Does the CEO possess the right background in banking?[3]
- Are the board executives actually challenged in their decision making?

Other questions to address include the following: Is the board provided with sufficient and adequate management reporting, in accessible fashion, on the bank's performance and risk exposures? Are there controls built into the firm's culture such that they are adhered to when the bank's business strategy is in conflict with them?

The role of NEDs came under scrutiny in the wake of the crash. That some NEDs were not up to the standard required is evident. However, this should not detract from the vital function, in theory at least, that they do undertake. For one thing, business best practice dictates that the risk management function should report to an NED on the board. This clearly implies that the NED in question must be sufficiently experienced and capable. The national regulator should always interview the relevant NED to ensure that this person meets the standards required.

It is rare to observe genuine control at all levels of a bank that also boasts true innovation, creativity, and efficiency. It may be, for instance, that some institutions are simply too big to manage effectively, especially when things start to go wrong. However, this does not mean we should not attempt to implement an effective strategy at the top level and still maintain efficiency at the coal face. The bank crisis demonstrated that in some cases bank boards were not able to maintain effective control of the business as they expanded. Certain desks originated risk that went beyond the stated (or believed) risk appetite of the parent banks; in other cases the risk management department was marginalized or ignored, and at board level there was a rubber-stamp mentality. These instances have significant implications for bank corporate governance.

LIQUIDITY RISK MANAGEMENT

In the aftermath of the crisis, the UK Financial Services Authority (FSA) published *Consultative Paper 08/22* and *Consultative Paper 08/24* in 2008, the recommended requirements of which were formalized in its *Policy Statement 09/16* in October 2009. These documents have set a standard for bank liquidity management that is expected to be mirrored, in part if not in whole, in other jurisdictions around the world. As such they hint at a new facet of the basic bank business model, concentrated on the liabilities side of the balance sheet. In essence the FSA has recognized that the crisis of 2007–2009 was as much a liquidity crisis as a capital loss crisis, and acted to mitigate this risk going forward.

Liquidity Management: The New Model

The basic tenets of the FSA proposals are grounded in market logic. Their content is expected to become business best practice in due course, and bank boards and senior management need to incorporate them into their operating model. The salient points include the following:

- The number of mismatch (gap) limits were increased, as was supervisory oversight.
- International cooperation between regulators was increased.
- Bank liquidity reporting obligations and their frequency were increased.
- Certain behavioral adjustments that were previously allowed have been revoked or reduced, for example, intragroup committed liquidity facilities no longer count as automatic funding self-sufficiency.
- Other behavioral adjustments are to be reviewed on a case-by-case basis, for example, the treatment of the stickiness of deposits.
- There is a new requirement to hold buffers of truly liquid assets; this is discussed elsewhere in this chapter.
- There is a new requirement to increase the average tenor of funding and to diversify the sources of funds.

The main implication of these requirements is increased cost and, all else being equal, a lower ROE. Other implications for this new business model include:

- Greater level of senior management and board governance and responsibility.
- An improved liquidity risk management capability (including better use of stress testing and improved contingency funding plans).

- A decreased reliance on short-term wholesale funding.
- Greater incentive for a bank to attract retail time deposits and longer-term wholesale deposits.
- Higher amount and quality of liquid asset stocks (including a higher proportion held in government bonds): the liquid asset buffer.
- In theory, a reduced expansion of bank lending during favorable economic times.

The main implication for banks is an increased likelihood of their surviving a liquidity stress event.

Another aspect of the new bank model, required by regulators, is more in-depth and more realistic stress testing. Jurisdictions will differ in detail, but taking the FSA papers as an example, banks should implement the following three stress tests:

1. A name-specific shock.
   - Unforeseen name-specific shock.
   - Market perceives firm to be potentially insolvent in short term.
   - Long-term impact: severity of multi-notch downgrade in credit rating.
2. Marketwide dislocation.
   - Unforeseen short-term marketwide dislocation that gradually evolves into a long-term marketwide liquidity stress.
   - Widespread concerns about solvency of financial sector.
   - Uncertainty of value of financial assets.
   - Certain asset classes remain illiquid for a long period.
3. Combination of (1) and (2).

Using the FSA template as a guide, a bank should stress-test the following main risk drivers:

- Wholesale funding risk.
- Intragroup funding risk.
- Intraday liquidity risk.
- Cross-currency liquidity risk.
- Retail funding risk.
- Size and quality of liquidity buffer.
- Wholesale (unsecured) lending and retail loans.
- Off-balance-sheet liquidity risk.
- Continuation of business.
- Diversification of funding sources.

The responsibility for formulating the stress tests, ensuring that they are carried out robustly and at required frequency, and reporting the results

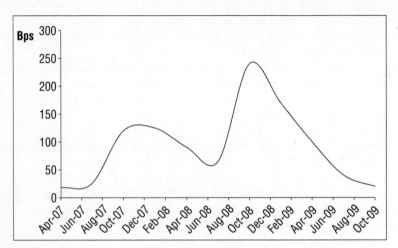

FIGURE 9.5   Sterling LIBOR-OIS spread, 2007–2009
Data source: Bloomberg.

to the board, lies with the chief risk officer. Under business best-practice culture, this person will report directly to an NED on the board.

Countercyclical Funding

One additional lesson learned from the crash is that banks should take advantage of benign conditions to improve their funding structures. Figure 9.5 shows the rise and fall in London Interbank Offer Rate (LIBOR) spreads during 2007–2009, giving an idea of the market conditions that may prevail and suggesting when a bank may wish to take on more funding to take advantage of LIBOR rates.[4]

In the first instance this would involve reducing the reliance on short-term funding. The definition of *short-term* is not universal; depending on which person one asks, it may mean up to one week or up to three months. Irrespective of the view that an individual bank takes, and this should reflect the bank's particular business model and current funding gap, best business practice suggests that a time of low funding spreads is the opportune moment to change the liability structure by increasing average maturity tenor. For instance, in the United Kingdom, overall banks had reduced their reliance on funding of up to one week from 15 percent of unsecured wholesale funding in December 2008 to 9 percent by October 2009. The aggregate customer funding gap (the difference between customer loans and customer deposits) was at £610 billion by Q2 2009, compared to £842

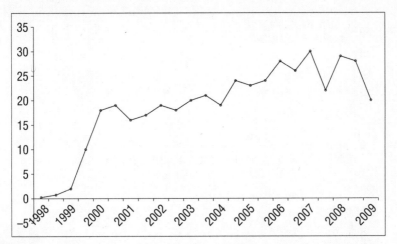

FIGURE 9.6   UK Banks Customer Funding Gap, 1998–2009, Median Value
Data source: British Bankers Association.

billion at the end of Q4 in 2008. This was 18 percent of all loans, the lowest proportion since 2003.[5] This is shown in Figure 9.6.

This is a critical feature of the new bank business model. The main lesson of the 2007–2009 crisis was the importance of liquidity risk management. To mitigate the impact of the next recession, bank funding structures need to be set up to reduce the reliance on short-term funding and unstable wholesale funding. They also need to extend the maturity of the liability side of the balance sheet. Excluding notable exceptions such as the banks in Australia and Canada, many country banks' customer funding gaps are uncomfortably high (see Figure 9.7). Banks must address the requirements, which are (1) to reduce the reliance on wholesale funding, which is not sticky and is less stable than retail customer deposits; and (2) to increase the average tenor of their liabilities. The UK bank sector, for example, remains vulnerable in this regard: The Bank of England reports that about 50 percent of UK bank aggregate wholesale funding is lower than six months in maturity.[6]

Bank funding strategy should therefore include targeting increased use of retail funding. Retail deposits are treated by regulators as being more stable, with greater expectation of being rolled over and not withdrawn on maturity. To reduce its funding gap (whatever it is), a bank would seek to grow its retail deposits.

At a tactical level, this raises the question of what interest rate to pay to attract more such deposits. Figure 9.8 shows the change in average spread

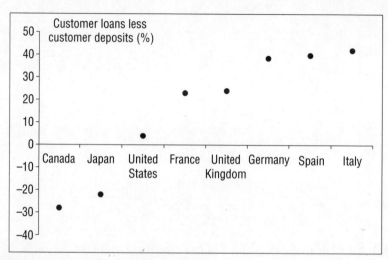

FIGURE 9.7   Selected Country Bank Funding Gaps
Source: Bank of England (2009).

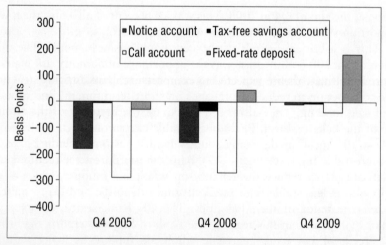

FIGURE 9.8   UK Banks Retail Deposit Spread
Source: *Money Observer* (www.moneyobserver.com).

on retail savings products offered by UK banks from 2005 to 2009. From a spread below LIBOR, the spread was increased to almost 200 bps over LIBOR. Partly this reflects the fact that absolute base interest rates had fallen to a very low level, but it also reflects the increased demand for such deposits from banks. It is important to pay a rate that is excessively above that in the market, partly for reputation reasons but also so as to not convey the impression that the bank is in difficulty and desperate for funds.

The overall impact of the new modified strategy will be higher funding costs. In adopting a more robust funding structure, there will be added costs associated with raising longer-dated liabilities (assuming a positive-sloping yield curve) and paying more to attract stable retail deposits. However, the object of this strategy is to reduce the vulnerability of the bank should there be another external shock or systemic instability.

The Basel Committee Proposals and the Net Stable Funding Ratio

The Basel Committee for Banking Supervision (BCBS) published extensive proposals for a revamp of certain aspects of the Basel rules, termed Basel III, for implementation from the end of 2012. In this section we consider the implications of its contents for bank liquidity funding arrangements and liquidity reporting.

A significant aspect of Basel III is a new liquidity measurement metric known as the net stable funding ratio (NSFR). The stated objective of the NSFR is to encourage more medium-term funding, and the metric itself highlights the level of long-term funding compared to short-term liabilities. At this stage, no limit for the NSFR has been set, and such a limit is unlikely; however, regulators are expected to compare each bank's figure against its peer group average and range. At the time of this writing, the exact calculation of the metric had not been specified; the authors agree with either of two suggestions put forward by the British Bankers Association (BBA) as part of its response to the BCBS proposals.

Certainly the NSFR is not a metric that one could set a one-size-fits-all limit on. As such, it is expected that supervisors will view it as part of a set of other metrics before determining regulatory compliance. However, bank senior management need to be aware of it and structure their liabilities to be within an acceptable bound for regulatory compliance.

The BBA has suggested either of the following definitions for the calculation of the NSFR:

- Capital plus term funding with residual maturity over one year plus non-wholesale funding, divided by assets not marketable within one year.

$$\frac{\text{Capital} + \text{term funding} (>1 \text{ year}) + \text{retail funding}}{\text{assets} > 1 \text{ year}}$$

- Given that the problem during the crisis has been one of overreliance on short-term (less than year) wholesale funding, an alternative calculation of the metric could be by using a formula of the form:

$$\frac{\text{Unsecured wholesale funding} < 1 \text{ year}}{\text{Total deposits} + \text{debt securities in issue} + \text{capital}}$$

In essence, the purpose of the NSFR is to control the level of maturity transformation that an institution undertakes.

With regard to liquidity measurement reporting, the BCBS has proposed a consistent set of monitoring metrics for all firms. The purpose of this is to assist supervisors across jurisdictions in looking at the liquidity risk in global banks, and create a common language, reducing the risk of misinterpretation of information by bank boards and regulators. It will also have the added advantage of reducing systems costs in reporting liquidity risk being run by such entities.

We discussed a range of reports in Chapter 8. Some of these are in the BCBS list. The authors of this book believe that a number of other metrics are also useful and have listed them here:

- Loan-to-deposit ratio.
- Cumulative liquidity model—a forward looking model of inflows, outflows, and available liquidity, accumulated for a 12-month period. It recognizes and predicts liquidity stress points on a cash basis. This will also include the one-week, one-month, and three-month liquidity ratios.
- Liquidity risk factor (also known as maturity transformation), the average tenor of assets to average tenor of liabilities.
- Interentity funding report for group and consolidated banking entities.
- Pricing data.
- Currency analysis.
- Retail and corporate funding levels.
- Long-term funding ratio/core funding ratio.
- Liquid asset buffer.
- Survival horizon.
- Domestic quantitative ratios.
- Systems and controls questionnaire or qualitative self-assessment.

Furthermore, the following management information reporting should also be produced for ALCO review (a one-sided A4 report summarizing all the following would be presented to the board):

- Funding concentration report, indicating extent of reliance on single sources of funds (e.g., top five biggest single sources, by sector and individual firm/customer, and whether within limits if the firm had set a limit of no more than, say, 10 percent of funds from one single source).
- Report on the amount of funding capacity that exists after taking into account the headroom required to survive a stress event (whether firm-specific or marketwide), the extent that existing liabilities and assets will be rolled over, and the amount of new business put on, over a given period of time. We call this metric the *surplus funding capacity* for a bank.
- Weekly qualitative report—a descriptive summary of any material detrimental changes to the preceding metrics. For example, this report could explain significant changes in one-week and one-month liquidity ratios, cash and liquidity gap in cumulative model, the liquidity risk factor, intergroup borrowing/lending position, and so on.

A bank that reports using the full suite of metrics listed here will be able to give a transparent picture of its liquidity position, which is essential to help ensure orderly regulatory supervision.

Bank senior management and boards must incorporate the elements of the BCBS proposals, which will be an essential element of the new bank model during the next 10 years.

THE LIQUID ASSET BUFFER

If one reviewed a bank balance sheet during the 1950s, and right up to the 1990s, it was common practice to observe that on the asset side part of it would be composed of government bonds. That this practice fell into disuse reflects the thinking of the past 10 years, that market liquidity could be taken for granted and bank liquidity portfolios could be held in the form of higher-yielding bank bonds (medium-term notes [MTNs] and floating rate notes [FRNs]).

Under the FSA *Policy Statement 09/16*, a "liquid asset buffer" (LAB) is now mandatory for all UK-regulated banks, and we recommend that it become a standard part of all bank business models, irrespective of jurisdiction, because of the obvious risk mitigation impact of so doing. Because sovereign bonds pay less than other securities, the implication of this change is clear: ROE will be lower.

Using the FSA requirements as our template, a bank should take the basic operating model for its LAB as follows:

- All firms are required to hold buffers of liquid assets.
- The expectation behind this thinking is that LAB assets will retain both value and liquidity in a stressed environment. The evidence for this is strong: In October and November 2008, the only assets that remained liquid, and acceptable for repo, were G7 sovereign securities. Bank CDs, FRNs, corporate bonds, and structured finance securities all became illiquid and/or were no longer acceptable as collateral.
- The central bank eligibility of the LAB asset is irrelevant; the FSA has specified assets eligible for the LAB.
- The LAB cannot be funded in repo, but must be funded by long-term (more than 90 days) funds, including retail and wholesale funds. This is to ensure that the bonds can act as a true buffer of liquidity, able to be sold or repossessed if funding becomes stressed for the bank.

The LAB for most banks in Western jurisdictions would be expected to be composed of the following (this is taken directly from the FSA document):

Highly liquid, high-quality government debt instruments such as gilts, plus bonds rated at least Aa3 issued by the countries of the European Economic Area (EEA), Canada, Japan, Switzerland and the United States; and

Reserves held with the Bank of England's reserve scheme and with the central banks of the United States, the EEA, Switzerland, Canada and Japan.

Designated multilateral development banks including:

- *African Development Bank.*
- *Asian Development Bank.*
- *Council of Europe Development Bank.*
- *European Bank for Reconstruction and Development.*
- *European Investment Bank.*
- *Inter-American Development Bank.*
- *International Bank for Reconstruction and Development.*
- *International Finance Corporation.*
- *Islamic Development Bank.*
- *Nordic Investment Bank.*

It is fairly clear that the LAB at a bank must hold ideally only high-quality assets, or otherwise be composed of cash deposits at the central bank. Because many eligible bonds held in a LAB would pay lower than LIBOR, banks will want to hold longer-dated such bonds so as not to lose money on the portfolio, if they are funded shorter tenor in a positive-sloping yield curve environment.

The FSA expects a firm to turn over its liquidity buffer on a regular basis, either through the sale of the assets or via repo. As we noted earlier, the portfolio cannot be funded in repo. It must be funded using unsecured funds, retail deposits, or other funds, and these must be term funds (that is, over 90 days to maturity). The size of the buffer is a key point. The exact proportion of a bank's balance sheet that has to be held in the form of a LAB is a function of the type of institution and the structure of its funding.

The FSA calculation suggests that a bank will have to hold the aggregate total of its three-month funding base as a liquid buffer. In other words, the more long-term funds a bank has, the smaller its buffer can be. Essentially, the calculation stipulated by the FSA on how much of a buffer a bank needs to hold is a function of how much shorted-dated (0- to 90-day) wholesale funding a bank has. The higher this amount, the bigger the size of the LAB.

CONCLUSIONS

A neutral observer of the world's economic system would conclude fairly quickly that the financial markets and banks are an indispensable part of the economy and of societal well-being. It is vital, therefore, that any regulatory system should incorporate the means of enforcing stability in the banking market. It should also allow for financial market innovation, because it has been largely through innovation that many of the benefits of finance have been made available to the wider population. But the key priority is effective regulation so that even if individual banks are forced into liquidation, market stability is maintained. In other words, regulation must seek to preserve stability but also recognize that the main business of banks involves taking risk: The act of maturity transformation, the cornerstone of banking, creates risk exposure.

Bank senior management and the board should accept that the institutions they run are a pivotal part of society, and in the post-crisis era will be closely regulated. Contributing to the stability of the market is as important an objective for a board, as is achieving shareholder ROE targets. To this end, an understanding and appreciation of market stability is vital. In the first instance, increasing bank capital levels is a necessary but not sufficient means to ensure a stable banking system: Liquidity management is as important. In this regard, the UK FSA's requirement that all UK-regulated banks must maintain a liquid asset buffer (LAB) is a correct one. Forcing every bank to invest a proportion of its assets in cash, central bank deposits, and liquid AAA-rated sovereign securities is the best insurance protection against future liquidity crises.

We believe that all banks should adopt this approach. The exact proportion of the balance sheet that should be placed in the LAB is a function of the liquidity gap that the bank runs and the diversity and security of its funding arrangements. But a form of LAB is best business practice and all banks should seek to have one in place. In itself this is not a new suggestion; a truly liquid portfolio was commonplace in banks around the world 15 or 20 years ago. However, banks started to unilaterally relax their own requirements and remove liquidity portfolios, or move them into assets that were not truly liquid (such as bank FRNs), to the point where such portfolios had become rare even in supposedly conservative institutions such as the UK building societies. It is evident that the prevailing orthodoxy has now reverted to its original one.

Bank boards should seek to simplify their capital structures, in the interests of transparency and investor comfort. The simplest structure may well be the most efficient, with a liability base comprised of pure equity, retained profits, senior unsubordinated bonds, and deposits. Deposits are part of the country's deposit guarantee scheme, so such a structure leaves no ambiguity about what stakeholders are at risk should the bank fail.

The nature of bank liquidity management has been transformed, although many of the seemingly new requirements in regimes such as those implemented by the FSA are more of a return to basics than actual new practices. The new bank business model for the next 10 or 20 years will incorporate these practices, with boards recommended to pay close attention to their bank's liability structure. The basic tenets of the new liability model are less reliance on wholesale funding, less reliance on short-term funding, a more diversified funding base, and genuine self-sufficiency in funding. Under this new model, banks will be considerably less likely to suffer failure at the time of the next market crash or systemic stress event.

Notes

Preface

1. An investor who held only risk-free sovereign securities such as Treasuries, gilts, or bunds would not have lost money during 2007–2008. But if this was done for risk-averse reasons then it is not actually a strategy as such, but merely the base-level risk-free option. If it was done as a directional play on interest rates, again this is not a value-added fund management strategy but is more akin to the tactics of the casino player. Either way, the fact that investors in risk-free sovereign securities made money during the crash reinforces our argument.

Introduction

1. The economist most closely associated with this description, and who predicted a crash of the sort experienced in 2007–2008, was Professor Hyman Minsky.

CHAPTER 1   Globalization, Emerging Markets, and the Savings Glut

1. This process is described in detail in David Smick, *The World Is Curved* (Marshall Cavendish, 2008).
2. Martin Wolf, *Fixing Global Finance: How to Curb Financial Crises in the 21st Century* (Yale University Press, 2009).
3. Frederic Mishkin, *The Next Great Globalization: How Disadvantaged Nations Can Harness Their Financial Systems to Get Rich* (Princeton University Press, 2006).
4. Michael Hutchison and Ilan Neuberger, "How bad are twins? Output costs of currency and banking crises," University of California working paper, January 2002.
5. P. Krugman, *The Return of Depression Economics and the Crisis of 2008* (W.W. Norton & Company, 2009).
6. Where M2 = money supply and V = velocity of money or the amount of economic activity given the money supply.
7. Krugman, *Depression Economics*.
8. Gerard Caprio, Daniela Klingebiel, Luc Laeven, and Guillermo Noguera, *Banking Crises Database* (World Bank, October 2003).

9. McKinsey Global Institute, *The New Power Brokers: How Oil, Asia, Hedge Funds, and Private Equity Are Shaping Global Capital Markets*, October 2007.

10. The average leverage factor of the hedge fund industry as a whole is estimated at 4. *Source*: McKinsey Global Institute, *The New Power Brokers: How Oil, Asia, Hedge Funds, and Private Equity Are Shaping Global Capital Markets*, October 2007.

11. McKinsey, *The New Power Brokers*.

12. Speech by Ben Bernanke at the Council on Foreign Relations, Washington, D.C., March 10, 2009.

13. Wolf, *Fixing Global Finance*.

14. Ibid.

15. Ibid.

CHAPTER 2   The Rise of Derivatives and Systemic Risk

1. McKinsey Global Institute, *The New Power Brokers: How Oil, Asia, Hedge Funds, and Private Equity Are Shaping Global Capital Markets*, October 2007.

2. Later on his successor, Ben Bernanke, explained this conundrum by means of a global savings glut.

3. H. P. Minsky, *Stabilizing an Unstable Economy* (McGraw-Hill, 1986).

4. Markus K. Brunnermeier, "Deciphering the Liquidity and Credit Crunch 2007–2008," *Journal of Economic Perspectives*, Winter 2009.

5. Warren Buffett, Berkshire Hathaway annual newsletter to the shareholders, February 21, 2003.

6. The letter was written on behalf of the senior managements of Alliance Bernstein, Bank of America, Merrill Lynch, Barclays Capital, Blue Mountain Capital Management LLC, BNP Paribas, Citadel Investment Group, Citigroup, Credit Suisse, Deutsche Bank AG, D.E. Shaw & Co., DW Investment Management, Dresdner Kleinwort, GLG Partners, Goldman Sachs & Co., Goldman Sachs Asset Management, HSBC Group, ISDA Inc., JPMorgan Chase, Managed Funds Association, Morgan Stanley, PIMCO, Royal Bank of Scotland Group, Asset Management Group of the Securities Industry and Financial Markets Association, Société Générale (Soc. Gen.), UBS AG, Wachovia Bank, and Wellington Mgmt. Company.

7. This letter was also sent to the board of governors of the Federal Reserve System, Connecticut State Banking System, Federal Deposit Insurance Corporation, Federal Reserve Bank of Richmond, French Secretariat Générale de la Commission Bancaire, German Federal Financial Supervisory Authority, New York State Banking Department, Office of the Comptroller of the Currency, Securities and Exchange Commission, Swiss Financial Market Supervisory Authority, and UK Financial Services Authority.

8. Letter to William C. Dudley, president of the Federal Reserve of New York, June 2, 2009.

9. www.bis.org.
10. Myron Scholes' interview on CNBC, October 16, 2009.
11. Hernando de Soto, *The Mystery of Capital: Why Capitalism Triumphs in the West and Fails Everywhere Else* (Basic Books, 2000).

CHAPTER 3   The Too-Big-to-Fail Bank, Moral Hazard, and Macroprudential Regulation

1. This is noted in George Cooper, *The Origin of Financial Crises: Central Banks, Credit Bubbles and the Efficient Market Fallacy* (Harriman House Ltd., 2008).
2. FSA, Policy Statement 09/16, October 2009.
3. It is noteworthy that the chief executive officers of the last two firms had backgrounds in retail and not banking.
4. The liquidity ratio is essentially the asset-liability gap. A good idea of this gap can be determined by calculating the ratio of average maturity of assets to average maturity of liabilities. A higher ratio is indicative of a higher gap and higher liquidity or funding rollover risk.
5. Bank of England, *Financial Stability Report*, Issue No. 26, December 2009.
6. Lehman Brothers was capitalized at 11 percent at the time of its collapse, a level that was acceptable to regulatory authorities while it was still in operation.

CHAPTER 4   Corporate Governance and Remuneration in the Banking Industry

1. See the summary of U.S. corporate scandals, which suggests that this issue was far from an isolated one, at the Forbes web site, www.forbes.com/2002/07/25/accountingtracker_print.html.
2. Centre for Economics and Business Research, Quarterly Bulletin, October 2006.
3. Wealth was measured by the authors as the total package existing of salary, annual bonus, expected discounted value of future salaries, market value of stocks and stock options allocated to the CEO, amounts paid to the CEO under the long-term incentive program, other benefits such as 401(k) contributions, debt forgiveness, tax reimbursements, and guaranteed bonuses at inception.
4. This payment has been called a *malus*, as opposed to a bonus, at one bank that has adopted the system. The authors use the same term.

CHAPTER 5   Bank Capital Safeguards: Additional Capital Buffers and Reverse Convertibles

1. See Longmei Zhang, "Bank Capital Regulation, Lending Channel and Business Cycles," Institute for Monetary and Financial Stability, Goethe University, Frankfurt, March 2009.

2. See *Risk* magazine's interview with José María Roldán, director-general of banking regulation at the Banco de España, July 28, 2009.

3. Gary H. Stern, "Addressing the Too Big to Fail Problem," testimony before the U.S. Senate Committee on Banking, Housing and Urban Affairs, Washington, D.C., May 6, 2009.

4. Mark J. Flannery, "No Pain, No Gain? Effecting Market Discipline via 'Reversed Convertible Debentures,'" University of Florida, working paper, November 2002.

5. Note that the conversion will only be executed at maturity if the potential obligation is above the price of the stock at maturity. For example, an RC with a strike price of 80 while the underlying stock is trading at 90 will not be converted. An RC with a strike price of 80 while the underlying stock is trading at 70 will be converted.

6. Described in detail in (among others) J. Hull, *Options, Futures, and Other Derivatives* (Prentice-Hall, 2005).

7. B. Goldman, H. Sosin, and M. A. Gatto, "Path Dependent Options: Buy at the Low, Sell at the High," *Journal of Finance*, 1979, S.1111–1127.

8. Tze Leung Lai, Tiong Wee Lim, "Efficient valuation of American floating strike look-back options," Department of Statistics, Stanford University and Department of Statistics and Applied Probability, National University of Singapore, 2004.

CHAPTER 6   Economic Theories under Attack

1. See Martin Wolf, *Fixing Global Finance: How to Curb Financial Crises in the 21st Century* (Yale University Press, 2009); and Paul Krugman, *The Return of Depression Economics and the Crisis of 2008* (W.W. Norton & Company, 2009).

2. See also David Smick, *The World Is Curved: Hidden Dangers to the Global Economy* (Marshall Cavendish, 2008).

3. These thoughts are also shared by Jeroen de Smet PhD, head of Structured Credit at ING Bank in Brussels.

4. See the original exposition in Eugene Fama, "Random Walks in Stock Market Prices," *Financial Analysts Journal* 51, No. 1, September–October 1965.

5. This anecdote is recounted in Roger Lowenstein, *When Genius Failed: The Rise and Fall of Long-Term Capital Management* (Random House, 2000).

6. Author's conversation with Jeroen de Smet.

7. Ibid.

8. See D. Kahneman's paper, "Maps of Bounded Rationality: A Perspective on Intuition Judgment and Choice," *American Economic Review*, 2003, 1,449–1,475.

9. John Mauldin, *Six Impossible Things before Breakfast*, weekly newsletter, August 7, 2009.

10. The analysis was done on U.S. growth and value stocks over the period 1950–2008.
11. J. Michael Murphy, "Efficient Markets, Index Funds, Illusion and Reality," *Journal of Portfolio Management* 5, No. 22 (Fall 1977).
12. Jeroen de Smet (ibid).
13. Anne P. Villamil, "The Modigliani-Miller Theorem," *The New Palgrave Dictionary of Economics* (University of Illinois, 2004).
14. F. Modigliani and M. H. Miller, "The Cost of Capital, Corporate Finance and the Theory of Investment," *American Economic Review* 48 (1958): 261–297.
15. See H. M. Markowitz, "Portfolio Selection," *Journal of Finance*, 1952, 77–91.
16. Jonathan Lewellen, "Institutional Investors and the Limits of Arbitrage," Dartmouth College and NBER, working paper, February 2009.
17. *McKinsey Quarterly*, interview with Nassim Taleb, December 2008.
18. See Hyman P. Minsky, *Stabilizing an Unstable Economy* (Yale University Press, 2008).
19. Ibid., 194.
20. Gerald O'Driscoll Jr., "Asset Bubbles and Their Consequences," Cato Institute, May 2008.
21. Minsky, *Stabilizing*, 272.
22. Lawrence G. McDonald and Patrick Robinson, *A Colossal Failure of Common Sense: The Inside Story of the Collapse of Lehman Brothers* (Crown Business, 2009).

CHAPTER 7   Long-Term Sustainable Investment Guidelines

1. McKinsey Global Institute, "Debt and Deleveraging: The Global Credit Bubble and Its Economic Consequences," January 2010.
2. Bill Gross, "The Ring of Fire," PIMCO newsletter, January 2010.
3. Carmen Reinhart and Kenneth Rogoff, *A Panoramic View of Eight Centuries of Financial Crises* (Harvard University, April 2008).
4. Ibid. 5.
5. See also www.givanomics.com, "Aging Societies and Public Finances," February 2010.
6. IMF, "The State of Public Finances: Outlook and Medium Term Policies After the 2008 Crisis," March 2009.
7. Barclays Capital, "Equity Gilt Study 2010," January 2010.
8. C. Reinhart and K. Rogoff, "Growth in a Time of Debt," Harvard University, December 2009.
9. Mohamed El-Erian, "Secular Outlook: A New Normal," PIMCO newsletter, May 2009.
10. Milton Friedman, Interview in *New Perspectives Quarterly* magazine, December 2005.

11. Henry M. Paulson, "On the Brink: Inside the Race to Stop the Collapse of the Global Financial System," *Business Plus*, January 2010.
12. Standard & Poor's, "In the Long Run, We Are All in Debt: Aging Societies and Sovereign Ratings," June 2005.
13. Minsky, H., *Stabilizing an Unstable Economy* (Yale University Press, 1986).
14. Thomas Friedman, *The World Is Flat: A Brief History of the Twenty-First Century* (Picador, 2005).
15. Note that absolute inflation started to drop in the 1980s due to the aggressive stance of the Federal Reserve under former Chairman Paul Volcker, but cumulative inflation kept on rising.
16. See www.goldmoney.com.

CHAPTER 8   Bank Asset-Liability and Liquidity Risk Management

1. In continental European banks they appear to prefer retaining the term *mismatch* rather than *gap*.
2. This report is discussed in full in the case study in Choudhry (2007).
3. The reasons can be macro-level ones, affecting most or all market participants, or more firm- or sector-specific. The former might be a general market correction that causes the supply of funds to dry up, and would be a near-catastrophic situation. The latter is best illustrated with the example of Barings plc in 1995: When it went bust overnight due to large, hitherto covered-up losses on the Simex exchange, the supply of credit to similar institutions was reduced or charged at much higher rates, albeit only temporarily, as a result.
4. Such assets would be very short-term, risk-free assets such as Treasury bills.
5. It can, of course, lock in future funding rates with forward-starting loans, which is one way to manage liquidity risk.
6. Of course, the opposite applies. The gap risk refers to an excess of liabilities over assets.
7. Note that this terminology is not a universal convention.
8. Many bank assets, such as residential mortgages and credit-card loans, are repaid before their legal maturity date. Thus the size of the asset book is constantly amortizing.
9. The firm's capital will be invested in risk-free assets such as government Treasury bills or, in some cases, bank CDs. It will not be lent out in normal banking operations because the ALM desk will not want to put capital in a credit-risky investment.
10. In addition, the bank will be able to raise funds at LIBID, or at worst at LIMEAN, while it should be able to receive LIBOR in interbank-credit-quality assets.
11. New business will follow a long process of approval, typically involving all the relevant front-, middle-, and back-office departments of the bank and culminating in a "new products committee" meeting at which the proposed

new line of business will be either approved, sent back to the sponsoring department for modification, or rejected.

12. For example, a bank may have the "overnight" time bucket on its own, or incorporate it into an "overnight to one-week" period. Similarly, banks may have each period from 1 month to 12 in their own separate buckets, or may place some periods into combined time periods. There is not one correct way.

13. This section is an extract from the book *The Principles of Banking*, written by Moorad Choudhry and published by John Wiley & Sons (Asia) Pte Lt in 2010. Reproduced with permission.

14. FSA, *Policy Statement 09/16*, October 2009.

15. See FSA CP 08/22, page 23, "Strengthening Liquidity Standards," December 2008.

16. A. Blundell-Wignall and P. Atkinson, "The Sub-Prime Crisis: Causal Distortions and Regulatory Reform," OECD working paper, July 2008.

CHAPTER 9   A Sustainable Bank Business Model: Capital, Liquidity, and Leverage

1. Without naming the banks, the authors are aware of institutions that purchased asset-backed securities (ABSs) and collateralized debt obligations (CDOs) with the belief that the senior tranche, rated AAA, would not be downgraded even if there was a default in the underlying asset pool, presumably because the junior note(s) would absorb the losses. Of course, this loss of subordination does erode the initial rating of the senior note, with a consequent mark-down in market value. Another institution, according to anecdotal evidence received by e-mail, entered into negative basis trades without any consideration for the funding cost of the trade package. This resulted in losses irrespective of the performance of the basis. In this case, it is clear that the trading desk in question entered into a relatively sophisticated trading strategy without being sufficiently aware of the technical implications.

2. See Bank of England (2009).

3. The CEOs of two failed British banks, HBOS and Bradford & Bingley plc, had backgrounds in retail and not banking.

4. See Chapter 10 in Choudhry (2007), which discusses the fair value of the LIBOR term premium.

5. See Bank of England (2009).

6. Ibid.

References

Acharya, Viral V., and Matthew Richardson. 2009. *Restoring Financial Stability: How to Repair a Failed System*. Hoboken, NJ: John Wiley & Sons.

Bank of England. 2009. The role of macroprudential policy. *Financial Stability Report* 25, November.

———. 2009. *Financial stability report* 26, December.

Bernanke, Ben. 2007. "Financial Regulation and the Invisible Hand." Remarks at the NY University Law School, April 11.

Brunnermeier, Markus K. 2009. Deciphering the liquidity and credit crunch 2007–2008. *Journal of Economic Perspectives*, Winter.

Caprio, Gerard, Daniela Klingebiel, Luc Laeven, and Guillermo Noguera. 2003. *Banking Crises Database*. Washington, DC: World Bank, October.

Centre for Economics and Business Research. 2006. *Quarterly Bulletin*, October.

Choudhry, M. 2005. *Fixed Income Markets*. Singapore: John Wiley & Sons (Asia) Pte Ltd.

Choudhry, M. 2007. *Bank Asset and Liability Management*. Singapore: John Wiley & Sons (Asia) Pte Ltd.

Choudhry, M. 2009. A clearing house for the money market? *Europe Arab Bank Treasury Market Comment* 1 (9) (March 6).

Cooper, George. 2008. *The Origin of Financial Crises: Central Banks, Credit Bubbles and the Efficient Market Fallacy*. Hampshire, UK: Harriman House Ltd.

Financial Services Authority. 2008. Consultative paper 08/22, December.

Hutchison, Michael, and Ilan Neuberger. 2002. How bad are twins? Output costs of currency and banking crises. University of California working paper, January.

Krugman, Paul. 2009. *The Return of Depression Economics and the Crisis of 2008*. New York: W.W. Norton & Company Ltd.

McDonald, Lawrence G., and Patrick Robinson. 2009. *A Colossal Failure of Common Sense: The Inside Story of the Collapse of Lehman Brothers*. New York: Crown Business.

Rogoff, K., and Reinhart, C. 2008. "This Time Is Different: A Panoramic View of Eight Centuries of Financial Crises," National Bureau of Economic Research working paper No. 13882, March.

Sorkin, Andrew Ross. 2009. *Too-Big-to-Fail: The Inside Story of How Wall Street and Washington Fought to Save the Financial System and Themselves*. New York: Viking Penguin.

Wolf, Martin. 2009. *Fixing Global Finance: How to Curb Financial Crises in the 21st Century*. New Haven, CT: Yale University Press, 2009.

About the Authors

Moorad Choudhry has over 21 years' experience in investment banking and was latterly head of treasury at Europe Arab Bank in London. He is a visiting professor at London Metropolitan Business School; a visiting research fellow at the ICMA Centre, University of Reading; a fellow of the *ifs*-School of Finance; a fellow of the Global Association of Risk Professionals; a fellow of the Institute of Sales and Marketing Management; and a fellow of the Chartered Institute for Securities and Investment. He is on the editorial board of the *Journal of Structured Finance* and on the editorial advisory board of the American Securitization Forum.

Gino Landuyt is head of institutional sales at Conduit Capital Markets in London. Prior to that he was head of treasury sales at Europe Arab Bank in London, head of mid-cap institutional structured sales at ING Bank in Brussels, and in sales and origination at KBC Bank NV in their Brussels, Frankfurt, New York, and London offices. Gino has an MA in applied economic sciences from the State University of Antwerp, and an MBA from St. Ignatius University in Antwerp.

Index

0 1341 1321455 2

RECEIVED

JUN 03 2011

HUMBER LIBRARIES
LAKESHORE CAMPUS